THE ART OF
REFLECTIVE
TEACHING

THE ART OF

REFLECTIVE TEACHING

PRACTICING PRESENCE

CAROL R. RODGERS

TEACHERS COLLEGE PRESS

TEACHERS COLLEGE | COLUMBIA UNIVERSITY

NEW YORK AND LONDON

Published by Teachers College Press,® 1234 Amsterdam Avenue, New York, NY 10027

Cover photo by Bychykhin_Olexandr / iStock by Getty Images.

Chapter 3 contains excerpts from "Seeing Student Learning: Teaching Change and the Role of Reflection," by C. Rodgers, 2002, *Harvard Educational Review*, 72(2), pp. 230–253. Reprinted with permission.

The poem "miss rosie" from *The Collected Poems of Lucille Clifton*, by Lucille Clifton, is reprinted with permission of The Permissions Company, LLC on behalf of BOA Editions, Ltd., boaeditions.org. Copyright © 1969, 1987 by Lucille Clifton.

Library of Congress Cataloging-in-Publication Data

Names: Rodgers, Carol Richardson, author. | Teachers College Press.
Title: The art of reflective teaching : practicing presence / Carol R. Rodgers.
Description: New York : Teachers College Press, 2020. | Includes bibliographical
    references and index. | Summary: "This book examines what it means to be
    present in one's teaching—how to mentally and emotionally connect to your
    students, your classroom, and your teaching. The author outlines the structure
    of reflection, its intentional practice, and its importance to presence. Rodgers
    also provides a detailed outline for teaching presence to new and preservice
    teachers"— Provided by publisher.
Identifiers: LCCN 2019057716 (print) | LCCN 2019057717 (ebook) | ISBN
    9780807763643 (Paperback : acid-free paper) | ISBN 9780807763650
    (Hardcover : acid-free paper) | ISBN 9780807778463 (eBook)
Subjects: LCSH: Reflective teaching. | Teachers—Training of.
Classification: LCC LB1025.3 .R626 2020 (print) | LCC LB1025.3 (ebook) | DDC
    371.102—dc23
LC record available at https://lccn.loc.gov/2019057716
LC ebook record available at https://lccn.loc.gov/2019057717

ISBN 978-0-8077-6364-3 (paper)
ISBN 978-0-8077-6365-0 (hardcover)
ISBN 978-0-8077-7846-3 (ebook)

Printed on acid-free paper
Manufactured in the United States of America

For my family,
my heart's home and my best and most beloved teachers,
and my SIT colleagues, fellow seekers all

Contents

Acknowledgments

When picking up a new book, I turn to the Acknowledgments to read the author's story: the marathon they have run, with gratitude to the team that made it possible. I am grateful to so many of those companions. The seed of this book was planted in 2006 when Miriam Raider-Roth and I wrote the original article, "Presence in Teaching." Miriam's support for the publication of this book was generous and full, and I thank her. Since the publication of that article, teachers have confirmed the importance of the idea of presence in their teaching. Their desire for more inspired this book.

This book is dedicated in part to my former SIT (School of International Training) colleagues, now dispersed but, as I say, seekers all. My SIT companions Jack Millett, Claire Stanley, Leslie Turpin, Marti Anderson, Bev Burkett, Pat Moran, and Sean Conley have provided a home for inquiry into my practice and "life," which, it turns out, are one in the same. Jack and Claire, cofounders of the Vermont Insight Meditation Center, have been guides and sounding boards in my forays into mindfulness. Mostly, they have modeled it. I thank them from the bottom of my heart for their friendship and wisdom. Claire read every word of this book and gave me just the right kind of feedback—critique that made me want to keep on writing.

My entire family has seen me through this process. My sister, Marta Hunt, a nurse who works with new mothers, reflected back to me the understanding of a teacher from a field other than education. She, too, knew how to fuel my energies while pointing out where they were misdirected. My daughter, Liz, read drafts with a loving, careful, and uninhibited eye. She makes me laugh every day and is a brilliant teacher; being able to talk shop with her brings me great joy. My "sun," Jon, has beamed love and encouragement throughout. My stepdaughter, Melissa, and her family, Felix, Zola, and Victor, posed real questions that made me feel that my work mattered. My husband, Jim, has cooked me meals, poured me wine, supported my absence through two writing retreats, and vacationed with a working wife. He has read every word with his incomparable editor's eye, and he's been my stalwart. Without him this journey would never have begun.

Preface

Why I Wrote This Book

[A philosophic attitude is] a distinguishing characteristic of humans everywhere since time immemorial—or there would be no myths of origin and struggle, no philosophies of knowledge, no metaphysical philosophies in search of ultimate answers, and so on. And, equally, returning again to daily life, there would be no philosophies particular to our personal lives—the values and creeds by which we live, tested and retested in experience—without which, or should they fail us, we suffer the pain of being without anchor, adrift, bereft, a plaything of fate.

—Patricia Carini, 2010

ORIGINS

In many ways, this book is a statement of my philosophy of teaching. We ask new teachers to write statements of their philosophy of teaching as they leave their teacher education programs or apply for jobs. But philosophies are both hewn in and tempered by experience. If I had written one in the 1970s, it would have been much different from what I now consider to be my philosophy of teaching. It is also a learning statement—how my experiences have hewn and tempered me. Thus, it is filled with many personal stories and stories from my students, rendered into a philosophy. My hope is that it will be of use to you, whether you are a new teacher or a veteran teacher, a teacher educator or a school board member, happy or unhappy with the state of education.

Teachers often draw a dark picture of the constraints "the system" places on them. They frequently invoke these fetters (high-stakes tests, teacher assessments, scripted curricula) as explanations for what can't be done. And there is no denying the pressure of these constraints. Testing has reached all the way down into kindergarten, and recess time has been squeezed out in favor of more classroom time. Many a teacher has left the profession and others have decided not to enter it because of these constraints. All this is true. And yet . . .

Even in the highly regulated halls of school, there is light that manages to shine through the cracks. These "discretionary spaces" (Ball,

2018)—pedagogical interstices where a teacher still has choices about how to respond to students and situations—are there, no matter how small they may seem. This is a book about the choices we can make as teachers and teacher educators in those cracks of light. It explores not just "moves" but how we can position ourselves internally to be more alert to—more present in—those discretionary spaces that happen in classrooms hundreds of times a day.

This is a book about learning to recognize and seize these opportunities, to give shape and meaning to the apparent chaos of internal and external forces and interactions that constitute a classroom, and to respond in ways that deepen and extend meaning for each person in that room and, ultimately, outside that room, in society, with the belief that doing so matters. Being present requires more than a set of dispositions, even though it requires certain of these; it is more than knowing students, although it requires this; it is more than subject matter knowledge, which it also requires. It is about seeing fully and responding with heart and intelligence. It is about seeing not just the learning, but the learner—her brilliance, her goodness, and her value to the world.

I have been teaching and working with teachers since 1977 and have been extraordinarily lucky in my career. I have taught children, young adults, and older adults. I have taught middle and high school boys in Sénégal with the Peace Corps; teens in a language institute in Washington, DC; public middle school students in Portland, Maine; Cambodian and Vietnamese refugees in resettlement camps in Indonesia; and pre- and inservice teachers in Vermont, Japan, and New York. I have supervised teachers in Mexico, Japan, Costa Rica, the Virgin Islands, Switzerland, Spain, and across the United States. I spent a year in South Africa as a Fulbright Scholar working with faculty in a newly integrated Faculty of Education and traveled South Africa's Eastern Cape to hear teachers' stories of humanizing, dehumanizing, and healing educational experiences. I currently work with a public charter elementary school in the Bronx and as an associate professor at the School of Education at the State University of New York.

I love to teach, in spite of the constraints in all of these systems. What remain central are my students and their learning. As I have navigated these contexts, I have learned that it matters to have a map and a good rudder to guide my practice, and touchstones by which I can test its strength and integrity. It matters to know, beyond meeting someone else's standards, what I am doing and why.

My teaching practice is guided by three big questions:

- How do I extend and deepen our mutual humanness?
- How must I work the soil of democracy in education so it will grow and sustain itself in the world?

- How do I connect learners to the natural world so that they come to care about and take care of it?

I know these are "lofty goals" and to some they will appear soft, nonspecific, and too grand to be of use. But when I walk a curriculum idea back to the reasons why or, conversely, ask what activities are suggested by these big ideas, they take on a specific character.

Connecting to big ideas goes beyond satisfaction with students' being engaged and on-task, or with activities that align with standards. How do these activities matter in kids' lives? Kids rightly ask, "When will I ever use this?" What do kids need now, not in some remote future? How is what we are asking them to do making their lives bigger, deeper, more interesting, more capable of contributing value to the world? How is it nurturing their becoming more compassionate and inquiring human beings? Is their sense of wonder and appreciation for the intricacies and beauty of the world growing or shrinking? How is our teaching strengthening the fragile state of our democracy? By what is our teaching anchored? How do we prevent our practice from becoming a thing "adrift, bereft, a plaything of fate," as Carini put it?

In asking, What does it means to be human? What is necessary for the survival of our democracy and the planet? I never reach the bottom of it all. There is always more to learn, about others, the world, and myself. I have found that reflection provides a process by which these questions can be kept in the forefront rather than periodically exhumed for the purposes of job applications or promotion. And I have found that the everyday practice of trying to stay present to the immense complexities of teaching gives me much to reflect upon. This is what I want my students of teaching to leave my classes feeling they can also do.

WHO THIS BOOK IS FOR

I have written this book for a wide audience: student-teachers; new teachers; veteran teachers; principals; doctoral students; teacher educators; those in professional development; other professionals, whose work—although not in schools—involves educating others; as well as the layperson interested in education. There are few professions where literally the entire population has been on the receiving end. After an average of more than 10,000 hours on one side of the desk, the layperson has formed strong opinions. I am hopeful this book can inform those opinions. But mostly this book is for teachers and teacher educators, to help unpack the complex world of teaching and to provide a common language to apply to felt experience as well as a reflective structure within which to use this language. It is also to help teachers stay in touch with why they went into teaching in the first place.

STRUCTURE OF THE BOOK

The book is divided into five parts, each comprising my own learning experiences and the thinking of writers and researchers who have kept me good company on that journey. Part I, Introduction to Presence, provides an overview of the philosophical underpinnings of presence as I define it, as well as my view of learning. Foundations include Maxine Greene's notion of wide-awakeness, contemporary notions of mindfulness, and Dewey's concepts of aliveness, perception, and recognition. In Part II, Defining Presence, I look at presence through five different lenses: attitudes of presence; mutual vulnerability; the permeable nature of self and world; inquiry; and love. Part III, What We Are Present to: I, Thou, It, and Context, uses David Hawkins's framework to further unpack and name the elements in play in any classroom, giving language and order to some of the complexities of the classroom. In Part IV, Reflection, I look at the process of reflection and discuss the relationship between reflection, presence, and mindfulness. Finally, in Part V, Educating for Presence: How Do We Learn to Be Present? How Can It Be Taught? I attempt to ground the ideas of the previous parts of the book in an online course I have taught for many years. I include six modules with activities, readings, lecture notes, and teacher-learners' voices.

I am continually learning and welcome feedback and questions from readers, my co-learners.

THE ART OF
REFLECTIVE
TEACHING

Part I

INTRODUCTION TO PRESENCE

As learners, many of us have experienced a teacher's presence. We have benefited from teachers who, attentive to us and our process, could give us exactly what we needed, neither more nor less, exactly when we needed it. From the learner's point of view, this moment is one of recognition, of feeling seen and understood, emotionally, cognitively, physically, or even spiritually. It is a feeling of being safe, where one is drawn to risk because of the discoveries such risk might reveal; it is the excitement of discovering one's self in the context of the larger world, rather than the worry of losing one's self in the process.

PHILOSOPHICAL FOUNDATIONS

Presence from the teacher's point of view is the experience of bringing one's whole self to full attention so as to perceive what is happening in the moment. Returning to the Latin roots of "attend"—to stretch toward—and "perceive"—to listen or pay close attention to; to accompany; to remain ready to serve—we find the kernel of presence.

In this introduction I look broadly at presence, beginning with three ideas that are foundational to my thinking: the concept of wide-awakeness, the practice of mindfulness, and John Dewey's concepts of aliveness, recognition, and perception.

Wide-Awakeness

While this is a book about reflection and presence in teaching, it is impossible to speak about teaching without also talking about students' learning. The state of alert attention described above applies equally to the learner and the teacher (also a learner). The learner is wide-awake to himself[1] and his life, and the teacher is wide-awake to the learner's mental and emotional states. She is also alert to the circumstances in which she has placed him, and the circumstances from which he comes that have shaped and continue to shape him.

"Wide-awakeness," a term educational philosopher Maxine Greene borrowed from Merleau-Ponty, points to being *in* the world, alert to the requirements of living, as opposed to being on the sidelines, learning about the world. It is grounded in lived experience and stimulates a quest for meaning. This wide-awakeness—a yearning to know the world and what it means—is what many progressive as well as conservative thinkers in education feel school should be about. Their means to this end may be different, but I believe it is a shared goal. Being in the world is certainly what childhood is about. I believe that being in school should be an experience of feeling more alive in, and connected to, the world, through one's own creation of knowledge of it.

Each of the basic disciplines we make children study in school—mathematics, science, literature, history—asks the same question: What does our world mean? Each discipline seeks to answer that question through its own particular lens. Mathematics sees patterns and predictability and the beauty of arrangements. The physical sciences trace Earth's physical story. Literature addresses the infinite ways we make sense of our experience of being human. History asks what our past means to our experience in the present. The disciplines open doors of perception, extending our human experience and expanding our selves.

I had a colleague, Vick, a professor of mathematics education, who said that she "saw the world mathematically" and wanted her students to experience the joy and aesthetic pleasure jolt she felt when seeing the patterns she saw in nature, in buildings, in numbers—to look out at the world and perceive its "mathematical-ness." Author Oliver Sacks's (1999) recollections of his childhood offer a further example. Sacks's Auntie Len was a schoolteacher who taught him Fibonacci number sequences by counting the patterns in sunflowers and pinecones. She taught him about the Golden Section and told him that the geometric proportions of pinecones and sunflowers were "the way God thinks." Numbers, he learned, "were not just delightful and friendly, but part of the plan on which the whole universe was built" (p. 62). At age 6, Sacks's parents sent him to boarding school, far away from the dangers of war in 1939. The school, however, was lonely and nightmarish. He was made to eat "swedes and mangelwurzels" (giant turnips and beetroots) and was regularly beaten by a vicious and sadistic headmaster (p. 59). In the midst of his misery, however, he managed to derive great comfort from the stability and predictability of numbers: "I liked numbers because they were solid, invariant; they stood unmoved in a chaotic world" (p. 62).

These stories illustrate what it means to be wide-awake as a learner. There is a parallel experience with a teacher as she "learns" her learners and how to teach them. She is wide-awake to them, their process, what they are learning, what preceded this learning, what comes next, and why it matters, all as it happens as well as before and after it happens. It is no small thing to be a wide-awake teacher, present to all this, and more.

Mindfulness[2]

Since the publication of our article on "Presence in Teaching" (Rodgers &
Raider-Roth, 2006), I have become increasingly drawn to explore—with
colleagues[3] and through the literature—overlaps between reflection and
mindfulness (which was mentioned briefly in that article). In my own practice of meditation, I have found great value in the "pausing" that this practice instills and see meditation as a highly effective tool for refining presence.
Moreover, I have found the principles that underlie mindfulness to resonate
with my view of presence and reflection. Indeed, the very word *presence* is
central to mindfulness practice.

The concept of mindfulness has been so popularized that one sees mindful coloring books and mindfulness apps, games, workbooks, and self-help
books. In what follows, I draw on the knowledge of expert practitioners
to give shape to my own understanding. One deeply appealing aspect of
mindfulness is that it is a practice grounded in one's experience rather than a
doctrine. Regular mindfulness practice, including meditation, is at the heart
of any conceptual understanding of it. Goldstein (2013) and others (e.g.,
Brach, 2012; Kabat-Zinn, 2015; Salzberg, 2011) underscore the fact that
presence is a state of being that results from regular "sitting," or meditation
practice, and that, although reading and a grounding in the precepts are
essential, mindfulness can be realized only through disciplined practice.

Mindfulness often is described in similar terms: presence, being awake,
and awareness. Sharon Salzberg (2011) defines mindfulness as "moment-to-
moment awareness." She writes that the practice of meditation "is essentially training our attention so that we can be more aware—not only of our
inner workings but also of what's happening around us in the here and now.
Once we see clearly what's going on in the moment, we can then choose
whether and how to act on what we're seeing" (p. 7). The key here is choice
and a considered, rather than reactive, response.

Jon Kabat-Zinn (2015) defines mindfulness as "awareness that arises by
paying attention on purpose in the present moment non-judgmentally. . . . [It
is] not a technique, but a way of being." He speaks of literally "coming to
our senses" (touch, taste, hearing, sight, smell)—waking up to our experience of these sensations in the moment, as they happen. Thinking is considered yet another "sense." Awareness, which attends to experience (including
the experience of one's thoughts) enters at the point of contact between
an object (like a sound or a thought) and the mind, and "holds [it] like a
mother holds a child." Echoing Salzberg's notion that mindfulness allows
for skillful choices, Kabat-Zinn states that mindfulness asks, "How can I
be in relationship with my thinking instead of reacting?" that is, pausing
before acting upon unconsidered assumptions. He notes that there is formal
practice (sitting) and informal practice (life), the former serving as practice
for the latter. Practice here is taken in the two senses of that word: practice

as the development of a skill, and practice as a form of spiritual discipline. "[Formal practice] means engaging in making some time every day to practice," he writes. "[Informal practice] means letting the practice spill over into every aspect of your waking life in an uncontrived and natural way" (Kabat-Zinn, 2016, p. 2).

Joseph Goldstein (2013) writes that mindfulness, simply stated, is "present-moment awareness, presence of mind, wakefulness, [which is] the opposite of absentmindedness" (p. 13). In a 2015 talk on "Mindfulness: What It Is and Is Not," Goldstein distinguishes between consciousness, mindfulness, and wisdom. Using the example of a Labrador retriever, Goldstein contends that even labs, with their boundless energy and curiosity, are conscious, or present—they read their world with staggering acuity of both smell and hearing. They are awake to the present, he says, but they are not "mindful." That is to say, there is no awareness of their presentness; there is no "observing power of the mind" or inquiry into experience. Mindfulness is distinguished by knowing that we know.

Goldstein goes on to explain that observation happens through affective "filters of the mind"—namely, aversion (e.g., anger, fear), desire (e.g., greed, pleasure), or delusion (e.g., boredom, not seeing). An awake mind is, he says, free of these filters or, more precisely, aware of these filters but not subject to them. In the moment that the mind notices that its thoughts have drifted toward reliving moments of pleasure, chewing over past injustices or regrets, planning, daydreaming, and so on, it frees itself, however briefly, from being subject to (dominated by) these states. It is practice that develops the "muscle" of mindfulness both to notice such attachments and aversions in the first place, and to prolong the momentary state of awareness and freedom. Thus liberated, the mind is free to choose "right" or ethical action. That is, awakening to these filters, and to the hidden motivations that color thought and direct action, gives us the freedom to choose "skillful" action. This he calls wisdom. An example—not of wisdom, I'm afraid—from my own experience follows. It is a story of awareness after the moment, rather than in it. I call it my "Pool Bitch" story.

I am a swimmer and regularly swim laps in a nearby pool. There are not a lot of lanes, often just three, and with just two swimmers to a lane, I sometimes have to wait. On one particular day, however, I was lucky and had a lane to myself. (I immodestly will admit to being a good lane partner. I don't splash a lot and I keep to my side. But when I get a lane to myself it's great. I don't have to worry about staying to one side or whacking my wrists on the hard, plastic lane dividers, and I can sail down the black lane line feeling rocket-like. I am, as is by now surely evident, a swim snob.)

When someone joins a lane it is customary to ask the swimmer already in the lane if they can join. On this day, a perfectly lovely average-sized man, about my age, asked if he could join me. It happened that, on this particular day, I had forgotten to put in my contact lenses and was swimming relatively blind. I thought there were other lanes open and, out of nowhere, possessed by the Pool Bitch who apparently lives inside of me, I said, "Can't you find an empty lane?" Understandably taken aback, he explained that all the other lanes were full. Before I could stop her, the Pool Bitch asked, "Are you a smooth swimmer?" (I still cannot believe I said this.) "Smooth enough, I guess," he offered, no doubt puzzled. I went on to explain, digging myself further into my unappealing hole, "You guys—men—splash and can take up a lot of room." "Oh, OK," he said, and started to walk away. At this point, now embarrassed and ashamed and fully awake to my appalling behavior, I blurted out an apology and urged him to share my lane. "I'm sorry," I said, "Of course, you are welcome to swim here." But it was too late; he had walked away and gotten into the hot tub where the nice people were.

I finished my mile, dragging shame and guilt behind me like ankle weights. By then the man had found an empty lane. I, desperate to shed these "icky" feelings and wanting to apologize again, leaned down to tap him on the shoulder. "I'm so sorry I was so rude," I said. "I really don't know what got into me." "It's OK," he said, and swam off down the pool. Just as I was about to enter the locker room, he stopped and called, "Do you really think it's a gender thing?" at which point we both laughed.

The point of this story is that my awareness, slow as it was to kick in, perceived my action as selfish and offensive, and knew it to be a reaction to men I'd experienced as "splash-y" swimmers seemingly unaware of the space their bodies occupied. A sort of pool-based manspreading. I had no evidence that this kind man was one of them, other than his maleness. I was judging an entire gender based on a few splash-y big guys! As soon as I realized this, I sought to repair the damage I had done. I would like to tell you that this was my last visit from the Pool Bitch. But it wasn't, of course. Still, I recognize her when she starts taking over with her snarky thoughts and can say, "Calm down, would you?" When I am more advanced in my practice, I suppose I will be gentler and kinder and more accepting of her as well.

Awareness of these feelings of judgment (of others and of myself) allowed me also to name them, to see them as thoughts, and to consider that while my thoughts can drive my actions, they are not me. In fact, for Buddhists there is no "me," no "I," no "self," only awareness. I can kind of see this, as it aligns with postmodern views of identity as shifting, multiple, and always in the making, but it is an insight that is a bit harder to grasp, and I am not the one to explain it, at least not yet. What I do understand is that, as tenacious as these feelings are, they are constructed, are impermanent, arise out of certain conditions, and do not add up to "me."

Because the person who teaches is also the person who swims laps, it matters to know her, to bring forth her best qualities, and to keep her worst qualities in check. Mindfulness practice has been useful in this regard. It is also useful in reminding me to be more patient with others whose selves are also in the making. Mostly, it has helped me to pause.

John Dewey

As a Dewey scholar and someone who has been deeply influenced by his work, I draw upon Dewey throughout this book. Part IV is devoted entirely to exploration of reflection and my interpretation of Dewey's work. Here I want to focus on his notions of aliveness, and perception and recognition, which are foundational to both reflection and presence.

Aliveness. In one of my favorite quotes from Dewey (1933), he describes embedded states of aliveness—by the student and the teacher:

> The teacher must have his mind free to observe the mental responses and move-
> ment of the student. . . . The problem of the pupils is found in the subject matter,
> the problem of teachers is what the minds of pupils are doing with the subject
> matter. . . . The teacher must be alive to all forms of bodily expression of men-
> tal condition—to puzzlement, boredom, mastery, the dawn of an idea, feigned
> attention, tendency to show off, to dominate discussion because of egotism,
> etc.—as well as sensitive to the meaning of all expression in words. He must be
> aware not only of their meaning, but of their meaning as indicative of the state
> of mind of the pupil, his degree of observation and comprehension. (p. 275)

In this quote Dewey talks about being alive and alert, and having one's mind free to observe. What I love about this quote is that it points squarely at this truth: The student is alive to the subject matter, and the teacher is alive to—present to—the student's encounter with the subject matter. The learner's aliveness comes from what Dewey refers to as his "active and alert commerce with the world." It is not the mere act of taking it in, he says, but interacting with it, meeting resistance in the form of puzzlement, difficulty, conflict with previous understandings, but persisting in the productive struggle of making meaning. Simultaneously, the teacher is engaged in the same meaning-making effort, but the object of her attention is the student and his encounter with the unknown. She must be present not merely to what he is doing but to what it means in terms of his "mental conditions," both embodied and verbal. Only then can she respond with the best next step. This dynamic is the act of teaching and one I return to throughout the book.

Recognition and Perception. I have found Dewey's (1934) distinction between two kinds of awareness—perception and recognition—to be extreme-ly useful in regard to presence in teaching. To merely recognize is to brush the surface of a thing only long enough to slot it into a category. "Mere recognitions," he writes, "occur only when we are occupied with something else [other] than the object or person recognized. It marks either an inter-ruption or else an intent to use what is recognized as a means for something else" (p. 24). He continues, "In recognition we fall back, as upon stereotype, upon some previously formed scheme" (p. 52).

In other words, we recognize something in the service of being able to move on, having successfully removed the problem by comfortably categorizing it. Recognition is a skill that admittedly serves us well in being able to move efficiently through our days, through the world. We learn what we need to pay attention to and what we can safely ignore. For example, when I was first learning to drive, I was taught that I needed to drive defensively. As a result, I was paranoid. Every driver coming toward me looked to me like an accident waiting to happen. It was exhausting. With time and a very patient father, I learned to recognize normal behavior and to relax, even letting my mind drift while at the same time being fully aware of the road, other drivers, my mirrors, and so forth. Teachers use this kind of awareness to keep order in a classroom, to spot and quell signs of disorder using a set of routine responses—stock phrases, take-a-break chairs, ritual claps, and verbal cues like, "Voices at level zero."

Perception, in contrast, involves suspending the urge to categorize and catalogue, staying with the object of attention long enough to allow it to reveal itself on its own terms rather than on ours. To perceive is to study and "take in," writes Dewey (1934, p. 53). Perception would demand that teachers resist the urge to label kids (recognition) based on selected behaviors and instead take in the whole of them. It is more than a passive, receptive process. It involves anticipation, engagement, inquiry, the active construction of meaning, and the formation of connections and relationships, on the road to seeing "the whole"—in this case, the whole of the person. (Of course, one is always only on the way, and never "there.") Recognition evades vivid consciousness, says Dewey. Perception, however, becomes "fresh and alive" (p. 53). David Hansen, in his soulful article "A Poetics of Teaching" (2004), hints at the necessity of perception and the art of teaching:

> The aesthetic aspect in teaching materializes . . . when a teacher is moved by the tapestry of human gestures, voices, strivings, and more, that come alive in any group of students. The teacher is affected by signs of grace, harmony, and beauty in-action, as well as by indices of frustration, rupture, and breakdown . . . the aesthetic dimensions of teaching and learning saturate their work—*if, that is, one has eyes and ears for them.* (emphasis added, p. 132)

He continues that the teacher, open to the human unfolding in front of her, can dwell in a place of beauty, a place where students might "shine." Like Dewey, Hansen touches upon the relational, moral dimension of perception. It is not merely to see but to serve the one seen. He elaborates: "Figuratively speaking, the teacher is drawn to every manifestation of human growth and development that comes within perception, and seeks to build upon them. . . . A way of perceiving fuses with a way of doing" (p. 135). Perception is employed to support the growth of a human being and to participate in that beauty, to stand in the light of that shining, be it scholastic achievement or the tenderness of a heart that has tried and failed.

PRESENCE

Taken together, these accounts teach us several things about presence. First, that it is a state of mind that is wide-awake and alert, filled with awareness. This open awareness anticipates nothing but is open to everything. It observes life's unfolding with curiosity and without wishing it were otherwise or shaping it to fit preconceptions. It also involves an awareness that is aware of itself. It is intentional. Presence as described here is in service not of itself, but of wisdom, that is, acting in the world in ways that serve. There is a moral dimension at play. It is, as Greene says, open to what is not yet, but might be. As such, it is an openness to the other and what they might become, and to the world and how it also might become. It is, for this reason, relational. It has an aesthetic dimension that bespeaks a vulnerability to being moved, touched, and changed. It is a natural state that also benefits from practice and discipline, and staying with.

I need to make one quick distinction: Being present and having a presence are not the same thing. The latter connotes an impressive bearing that causes others to sit up and take notice. Having a presence means that students' attention is drawn to the person teaching. This is not the kind of presence I mean. Being present means that the teacher attends to and is tuned in to the learner and the learning.[4]

MY VIEW OF LEARNING

I come to this book with a certain view of learning, which is unapologetically constructivist, but also aware that sociocultural, historical, political, and economic dimensions of power are always, always in play. I embrace the notion that all teaching is political, a notion that many teachers I work with object to, thinking that I am equating them with politicians. They don't like politics and want to distance themselves from such a notion. What I mean, however, is that all teaching involves dimensions of power, between people and contextually. Elements of power are always present, in oneself, in others, in the structures we all live in. Awareness of these dimensions is critical to teaching and acting morally in the world.

Teaching Is a Response to Learning

Fundamentally, I see teaching as a response to learning. While conventional wisdom and research indicate that good teachers are the most important factor in students' learning, it does not follow that because I am a good teacher

you will learn. In fact, we all learn many things without any instruction—
when we are newborns we learn how to nurse; to cry and make different
noises with our voices; to recognize faces; to roll over. Later, we learn how to
speak in sentences, crawl, stand, balance, walk, run, and so on. Later still, we
become proficient in discerning differences between humor, anger, and sadness; how to tell a joke; to infer; to perceive the existence of hidden objects.
All without being "taught." Clearly, we can learn without direct instruction.
But we also learn by being responded to, by getting some kind of feedback
that lets us know how things are going and what might need adjusting. If we
fall while learning to walk, we get feedback from that fall and the ground we
fall on. It's hard, it stops our progress, but it also doesn't kill us. We figure
out that we need to pick ourselves up and try again, differently. Nonetheless,
in order to make learning more efficient, to streamline the trial and error
process, we go to teachers and accept help, like parental hands that hold ours
and keep us from falling. Still, even the best teachers can only prepare the
ground for and support the learning, they cannot learn for us, as tempting as
that thought is. As one of my early mentors, Caleb Gattegno, used to say, "If
I eat, you don't get fat." In other words, if I do all the digesting, you get none
of the nourishment. But how many times have we as parents, as teachers, in
our impatience or exuberance, said, "Let me do it for you," or believed that
"telling" and "helping" cover the territory much more efficiently?

Because teaching is a response to learning, I as a teacher must be able to
perceive the learning in order to be able to respond with the best next step
in the learner's process, both cognitive and emotional. I must have created
a task and an environment that makes space for that learning to manifest
itself, and made provisions for my intervention should I determine, correctly
or not, that it is necessary. If there is more than one student, I have to think
about how I am going to set up the learning environment in a way that gives
me the best possible view of all my learners and their work, and opportunities to respond. It also may be that the best response will come from other
students, or that it may be no response at all.

If I am lecturing, I will see less. I can read faces, but what I see and my
interpretation of what I see may have little to do with what is going on inside the heads of my listeners. The more I give my students to *do*, the more
I can see (or hear) their thinking as it manifests in their actions and words.
Yet even then, what I see is only a partial view of what is going on "under
the hood." In other words, it takes a lot of careful planning, dialogue, patience, and attention to fully perceive the learning.

As I attend to my students' learning, I make decisions about where to
go next, which might be different for different people. This requires that I
make choices about who should move ahead, who needs re-teaching, who
needs to enter through a different portal, or whether I should completely
abandon what I am doing and go down a different path. All the while, I
must be mindful of a given curricular road map, especially if I am a teacher
in a public K–12 environment, but also at the college or university level.

A Word About Planning

Preparation may be as important as the actual teaching. It involves four things. First, knowing your subject matter deeply in order to have your mind "free to observe the mental responses and movement" of the learners. This knowledge is complex and never complete. It involves not just the facts but their multiple connections, including connections across subject areas. Second, it means preparing the space for learning. Is it a hospitable space, well-lit and clean, navigable? Is there color, beauty, even? (There is too little beauty in schools.) Are the seats arranged for conversation and interaction or only for listening? Is there fresh air? Even in depressing spaces, there are aesthetic openings that present themselves. In one school I know, teachers have strung Christmas lights that allow them to turn off the glaring overhead fluorescent lights. Sometimes classical music is playing softly in the background. A third leg of preparation is knowing—or building in a way to find out—what your students already know and can do. What is the edge of their learning? What knowledge can you build on and what is yet to be constructed? When students feel seen, trust can grow. Finally, there is the preparation of yourself, your state of mind, which is what the next part of this book is about.

Because I see teaching as a response to learning, it is imperative that I, the teacher, am present to that learning; present to myself and my own teaching, to my intentions and motivations; and present to both subject matter and larger purposes, both my own and those of the school and state. No one can be fully present to all these things, 100% of the time. There is too much, especially in a classroom, to be present to—too much to get done, too many problems to solve in the moment. There is no arrival point in teaching when we are the best teacher. We struggle toward full vision and a full response, but never achieve either completely.

Part II

DEFINING PRESENCE

CHAPTER 1

Attitudes

Certain attitudes open the way for presence while others occlude its possibility. In this chapter I speak of the former, assuming that those that fall into the latter group are their opposites. These positive attitudes include five that Dewey wrote about in the context of his exploration of reflective thought in *Democracy and Education* (1916) and *How We Think* (1933): directness, wholeheartedness, open-mindedness/nonjudgment, responsibility, and curiosity. I also have included the Buddhist notion of "equanimity" as a sixth attitude.

Dewey writes about specific attitudes that he considered necessary for reflective thinking and requirements for participation in a democracy. He speaks about these attitudes in the context of individual teachers' methods. Dewey notes that each teacher will have her own personal style but stresses that there are essential attitudes that all teachers must cultivate. The first of these is directness.

DIRECTNESS[1]

Dewey's (1933) definition of directness is different from our contemporary meaning of forthrightness or, even, bluntness. For Dewey, first and foremost, directness implies a kind of presence—not focusing on a particular end to the exclusion of being present to and trusting the value of what is. That is, "it denotes . . . unconscious faith in the possibilities of the situation. It signifies rising to the needs of the situation" (p. 181). It also connotes a lack of preoccupation with one's performance, especially in the eyes of imagined or actual others. Instead, one relaxes into a situation, trusting it. One is in a "whole-souled relationship" with the situation at hand; there is a kind of fusion between oneself and the situation.

I have speculated (Rodgers, 2002a) that perhaps teachers move through levels of directness as they gain expertise—from self-absorption, to forgetting oneself, to self-awareness. In self-absorption one is preoccupied in the ways Dewey describes—seeing oneself through others' eyes (students' eyes, evaluators' eyes, the eyes of parents, institutional and societal norms and expectations) and attaching the virtuosity of one's performance to one's sense of self-worth. Forgetting oneself involves a realization that "it's not about me," but about students' learning. Entering this stage can feel liberating. It allows for play, improvisation, full responsiveness, connection, and joy. I once wrote about my own experience of the starkness of this shift in awareness:

> I recall an experience I had in my days as a Peace Corps volunteer in Sénégal. There is a wind, which the Senegalese call the Harmattan, that blows off the desert from Mauritania. It is oppressive—hot, dry, and very, very dusty. My hair would lie flat on my head in thin, electrically charged strands; the red dust coated my eyes, nostrils, and throat. It coated every interior inch of my small apartment despite shuttered windows. It would blow for days; then without warning, the wind would abruptly shift. Instead of coming off the desert, it began to come off the sea. I felt as though I had walked through an invisible curtain. My hair seemed to double in volume, my skin became supple, and I could breathe again. The oppression of the heat lifted, replaced by the gentle lightness of the sea air. When teachers realize that teaching is as much a matter of response as it is invention, it can be startling. Rather than feeling the weight of who they think they *should* be, they begin to feel the gentle lightness of themselves. (Rodgers, 2006b, p. 232)

Self-awareness, the third level, demands a kind of dual perception, of students and their experiences in the moment *and* of one's own impulses and prejudices, coupled with the power to restrain oneself and stay open. A teacher who teaches from a place of directness will ask not, "How was my teaching today?" but, "Where was the learning?" The latter question depends entirely on a teacher's ability to observe and to be present, which is directly proportional to the degree to which she can be free from preoccupation. There is an authenticity to such teachers. They are comfortable in their own skin and connect with students with ease and humor without ever losing their authority.

WHOLEHEARTEDNESS

When I have asked students what makes a good teacher, they invariably cite enthusiasm and passion: a passion for the subject matter and also a passion for teaching itself. Good teachers find both of these fully absorbing, worthy of hours—or a lifetime—of tramping around in, digging into, wondering about in, investigating, and experimenting with. Dewey (1933) writes of what it means to be fully absorbed by subject matter:

> When a person is absorbed, the subject carries him on. Questions occur to him spontaneously; a flood of suggestions pour in on him; further inquiries and readings are indicated and followed; instead of having to use his energy to hold his mind to the subject (thereby lessening that which is available for the subject

itself, and creating a divided state of mind), the material holds and buoys his mind up and gives an onward impetus to thinking. (p. 32)

The contrast Dewey paints between trying to concentrate on a subject—you can almost hear the grunt of effort—and having the mind buoyed and moved, is both remarkable and deeply familiar. Who doesn't know the feeling of trudging through schoolwork or the rush of being carried away by wonder and curiosity? The subject matter of teaching, as we have noted, includes both the course material and students' encounter with it. The same wholeheartedness applies to each.

As with directness, wholeheartedness can be diluted by a desire to please others. As Dewey writes, "Amiable [or compliant] individuals want to do what they are expected to do," and the result can be a "divided state" where the deeper desires of the individual battle with the outward requirements. It is no giant leap to imagine K–12 teachers—and students!—most of whom enter teaching (or school) "wholeheartedly," feeling divided and beaten down by multiple requirements. One sign of the retreat of wholeheartedness is when teachers feel they must offer bribes or punishments to keep students on task; such teaching can feel like "pulling teeth." Likewise, the bribe of merit pay has never worked for teachers, just as the punishment of assessments based on students' test scores doesn't work either.

Although Dewey also referred to wholeheartedness as single-mindedness, no one would dispute that there is more than one thing to attend to in the classroom, and all of those things matter. In addition, there are internal dynamics to attend to, in oneself and in one's students. How to attend to it all and not be atomized? Vaporized? Dewey would, I believe, say that when the subject at hand connects to students, and the teacher connects to the students' learning, wholeheartedness is in play. I have seen students completely absorbed in figuring out how to represent $2/5 \times 1/2$ using Cuisenaire rods. It is a matter of figuring out the right task at the right time for the right student. One figures that out through experimentation and observation. When the students are doing the work, the teacher is free to be present to their sense-making.

OPEN-MINDEDNESS

The third essential attitude is open-mindedness. Dewey (1933) defined open-mindedness as "freedom from prejudice, partisanship, and such other habits as close the mind and make it unwilling to consider new problems and entertain new ideas . . . [and] to recognize the possibility of error even in the beliefs that are dearest to us" (p. 30). It includes a stance of "hospitality" to new ideas, suggesting a certain graciousness that welcomes them in, even if, at first glance, they may not be "your kind of people." Still, he says, it does not mean hanging a sign outside that says, "Come right in; there is nobody at home." Or, as Carl Sagan is reported to have said, "It pays to keep an open mind, but not so open your brains fall out." In other words, critical faculties are still in play. At the same time, the criteria for weighing what is valid and what is not must always be held open to question. Dewey (1933) warns that we can get so identified with an idea that we "rise to its defense and stop our mental eyes and ears to anything different." He notes that unconscious fears, like the fear of being wrong, can not only shut out new conceptions but also prevent us from making new observations (pp. 30–31).

Finally, Dewey (1916) reminds us that learning new ways of seeing is not necessarily a decision but a process of growth—it requires "a kind of passivity, willingness to let experiences accumulate and sink in and ripen." Such processes, he writes, "take their own time to mature. Were all instructors to realize that the quality of mental process, not the production of correct answers, is the measure of educative growth something hardly less than a revolution in teaching would be worked" (p. 183). Because these mental processes are unique to each individual, standardization is the enemy of open-mindedness, with, in Dewey's words, its "speedy, accurately measurable, correct results" (pp. 182–183).

An example of this mental (and emotional) process comes from my year-long experience in South Africa as a Fulbright Scholar in 2011. In my 11th month there, I wrote about some of what I was beginning to learn about gender oppression, religious oppression, racial oppression, and a humanizing pedagogy that sought to counter these forces. So much of what I learned arose from South Africa's oppressive histories and the realization that power, especially in a postcolonial context, is always in play. Although I had come far from the limited, sometimes arrogant, views with which I arrived, I sensed how very much I still had to learn. About teaching I wrote, "I am now beginning to see in stark ways that teaching has to be and always is a political act. Awareness is like a penny that sinks slowly through a vague and viscous knowing. When the penny finally 'drops,' you go, 'Wow, how did that take so long?' but I don't think there is any rushing it. It takes the time it takes, and then it keeps on sinking." It took a year for me to get to that point, with the help of patient, loving guides and teachers. While I arrived with wholehearted and open-minded intentions, there were still so many walls to knock down. There still are. Wholeheartedness and open-mindedness are indeed ongoing processes rather than states.

RESPONSIBILITY

Fundamentally, being responsible means taking one's own self and one's thoughts (even unconscious ones) seriously; that is, accepting that how one thinks and feels will play out in the world of people and events. In short, there are consequences. Buddhists call it karma (Goldstein, 2013; Olendzki,

2016). Responsibility means that one's intentions and purposes are exhumed and thought through to their possible ends. Integrity itself rests upon an attitude of responsibility. It is not hard to think of what happens when we refuse to take responsibility for our ways of thinking; global warming is, perhaps, the most pressing example of our time.

I turn again to my Fulbright experience for another example. While I am deeply uncomfortable with the notion of myself as racist,[2] I accept that I have been raised in a racist nation and am subject to its racist views. The unconscious racist views with which I arrived in South Africa had consequences. I recall a conversation I had with my host, Denise, one afternoon on our way to hear a school principal and former leader in the anti-apartheid struggle speak. Denise was explaining to me how "the 90% [Black, Indian, and Colored] struggled academically while the 10% [White] excelled." Embedded in her remark, but invisible to me, was knowledge of all the injustices that made this so. "So," I said ignorantly, "you want to get the 90% up to the 10%?" There was a long pause as, I imagine, she worked out how to respond to all that was embedded in my question. "No," she said slowly. "No, that is not how we need to think of it. We need to ask, What do the 90% have that we are not reaching and bringing forth? How do we value *that*?" If I had worked with the teachers I was there to work with—half of them from nondominant groups—with the notion that my job was to "bring the 90% up to the 10%," I would not have gotten far. Her response threw a harsh light on my limited point of view. I felt ashamed and embarrassed, but also grateful. Far better these feelings than the consequences of my own unexamined assumptions.

One of the reasons I was able to learn was that I was embedded in the South African culture, and with those who lived there, about whom I cared. Dewey states that when a learner's experience is too far separated from the subject matter, or when the facts are too numerous to memorize, it is more difficult to see the consequences of the ideas inherent in the subject matter. An indifferent shrug—"Whatever . . ."—overtakes responsibility for the consequences. When one remains untouched, indifference is easy. One of our jobs as educators is to create situations where learners feel touched.

CURIOSITY

I have never met a good teacher who was not curious—curious about the world, about other human beings, about the connections between us all. We are born curious, interacting with the world constantly to make sense out of it, asking why, touching the world, taking it in literally and figuratively, and making it a part of us. Curiosity is the energy that propels this reaching out into the world with all our senses, and such interactions constitute the framework of experience and learning (Dewey, 1933, p. 36). Dewey sees curiosity evolving through three stages. It begins from spontaneous interactions with whatever, to an intermediary stage of inquiry—"What is that?" "Why?" At this intermediary stage there is a sense that there is more to the world than what is visible; the world is a mystery to be unraveled. The final stage of curiosity is "intellectual." At this stage there is a more remote end that the learner has in mind. For example, one teacher, Eric, shared the story of his kindergarten students carving canals on a hillside on a rainy day. Their goal was to get the water to flow from the top of the hill to the bottom. But when they tried making the canal curve uphill, the water resisted their plans and overflowed the canal's banks. They had to figure out that water flows downhill, and that "downhill" comprises both directly downhill and also downhill-ish, which they did. Eric, a wise teacher, then extended their engineering victory into an elementary lesson about gravity. They solved the immediate experiential challenge of getting the water to stay in the canal, which Eric then "intellectualized."

If the teacher's remote goal is, for example, that learners understand the causes of World War II, and that they get curious about the causes of global conflict, her own curiosity might be around what it is that learners understand about conflict and power in the first place and how it affects them directly. She might then get curious about how to convert that understanding into a wondering about how power and conflict play out on a global scale. She has to avoid the impression that everything important about the causes of World War II has already been worked out and that the learner's only job is to remember those facts. Her job is to create an appetite for relevant facts—to till the ground for curiosity to grow.

Likewise, it is the teacher educator's job to "till the ground" for curiosity with new teachers, both at the level of subject matter (e.g., history) and the subject matter of teaching (pedagogy). If my desire as a teacher educator is to develop curiosity about children in teachers, how do I go about doing that? I have found that starting with the particulars of teachers' own stories of learning is a good way in. Part V of this book offers a curriculum for developing the kind of curiosity in new teachers that is essential to presence in teaching.

EQUANIMITY OR NEUTRALITY OF MIND

A sixth attitude, coming out of the mindfulness traditions, is equanimity or neutrality of mind. On her website Sharon Salzberg describes equanimity as "the ability to maintain a spacious impartiality of mind in the midst of life's changing conditions. A state of balance or poise; a radiant calm of mind or spacious stillness of heart" (Salzberg, 2019). My friend Claire, a meditation teacher, likens equanimity to surfing a wave.

While an equanimous mind is neutral and impartial, it is not indifferent. One of its characteristics is an acceptance of the vicissitudes of reality, namely, gain and loss, praise and blame, fame and disrepute, pleasure and pain. Rather than riding the rollercoaster associated with each of these shifting states, equanimity allows us to ride these waves, without being sucked into the roiling waters (Goldstein, 2013). "Its characteristic is evenness and when it is highly developed, it manifests as unshakeable balance of mind" (p. 277). Easy to say, less easy to do when, for instance, your students' test scores determine whether your district decides to tenure you. Essential to the achievement of equanimity, it seems to me, is the perspective that open-mindedness (acceptance of what is) and inquiry, both part of a daily meditation practice, provide. Equanimity results from practice, in both senses of that word—doing something over and over again until it becomes strong, and committing to it for purposes beyond strength itself.

CHAPTER 2

Mutual Vulnerability

I first heard the term *mutual vulnerability* in South Africa, where my colleagues André Keet and Denise Zinn referred to it in the context of a "post-conflict" society. Their article, "Mutual Vulnerability: A Key Principle in a Humanising Pedagogy in Post-Conflict Societies" (Keet, Zinn, & Porteus, 2009), views mutual vulnerability as a key principle of a humanizing pedagogy. Paolo Freire coined the term *humanizing pedagogy*, which falls within the larger frame of critical pedagogy. I first will look at these larger concepts— critical pedagogy and a humanizing pedagogy—linking them to presence, and then circle back to mutual vulnerability.

CRITICAL PEDAGOGY

Critical pedagogy takes as a given that formal education happens within historical, cultural, political, economic, and social contexts that exert force on its shape, content, and process. It acknowledges that all teaching is political in that it is inextricably intertwined with elements of power and oppression. Even very progressive schools are still subject to these realities. An example of one of these political dimensions would be the current "accountability culture" where tests, devised by large global corporations, determine the quantifiable "worth" of a community, a school, a teacher, or a child. Critical pedagogy holds that an awareness of these forces is the first step toward liberation from them. In other words, the project of moving from a position of being subject to these forces, to holding them as an object of inquiry and reflection, is the process of education. To use the language of critical pedagogy:

> As part of the meaning-making machinery, differences, interests and power relations are constitutive elements of cultural and normative frames. We refer to cultural and normative frames . . . as the "totality of background meanings, norms, discourses, and practices" to "which the self orients itself" (Odysseos: 2004, 5-6). (Keet et al., p. 109, 2009)

In other words, one cannot escape the reality of power differences in any culture or its institutions, which determine what is "normal." These norms exist as standards against which people (selves) measure their worth. They are established by and generally benefit those in power. But they are not givens, not laws of nature; they are constructed. Yet, the authors explain, the noncritical self (both oppressed and oppressor) orients itself to these meanings—accepts them as givens—advantaging those with power and disadvantaging those without.

Tara Brach (2012), a leader in the mindfulness movement, talks about moving from a position of "trance" to seeing "what is." Although she references mindfulness rather than critical pedagogy, the metaphor holds and illuminates a possible connection between critical pedagogy and mindfulness. Trance refers to being lost in the "story of oneself" and can be likened to being lost in a culture's story of "how things are." Here is a powerful example from education: Most Americans would not, today, question that the purpose of education is to prepare students for college and career, and to "grow the economy." Yet these purposes are relatively new and arguably serve large, corporate purposes more than they serve individual human beings or, collectively, a democracy. Most of us are in the thrall of this particular "trance" and do not question its rightness.

Moving from a trance state to a state of awareness is like moving from being inside a snow globe to being the person holding the globe, and seeing it as an object open to examination and critical thought. Psychologist Robert Kegan (1994) calls this moving from subject to object. One moves from being subject to one reality, one epistemology, to holding that reality, or way of knowing, objectively, as one among other possible realities. He writes that "transforming our epistemologies, liberating ourselves from that in which we are embedded, making what was subject into object so that we 'have it' rather than 'be had' by it" (p. 34) results from the experience of feeling that the present reality no longer "fits." In a sense, it becomes too tight and one needs to struggle out of it like a butterfly from a cocoon.

I am not referring here to multiple truths or "alternative facts," but to widening one's lens. Author Debby Irving, in her book *Waking Up White* (2014), describes her own dawning awareness of the cultural surround to which she had been subject:

> Just how far from the [white man's] "taming of the heathens" mindset was I really? When I got honest with myself, I had to own up to the fact that I'd bought into the myth of white superiority, silently and privately, explaining to myself the pattern of white dominance I observed as a natural outgrowth of biologically wired superior white intelligence and ability. Like a fish unable to recognize its surrounding waters, I'd never noticed the culture of white superiority in which I now understood I'd been soaking. (p. 44)

Awareness of the power structures to which one is subject, and the ways in which they either serve oppression or serve a more equitable and democratic society, is at the heart of a critical pedagogy.

HUMANIZING PEDAGOGY AND MUTUAL VULNERABILITY

A humanizing pedagogy seeks to address these "frames" by disrupting them. It was Freire's conviction that our purpose as participants in the ongoing, unfinished story of humanity was to become more fully human. "At all stages of their liberation," writes Freire (1970/2011) in *Pedagogy of the Oppressed*, "the oppressed must see themselves as women and men [and children] engaged in the ontological and historical vocation of becoming more fully human" (pp. 65–66). This kind of pedagogy speaks back to limited notions of education as a channel to college and career, and supports the project of becoming more fully human. This project belongs to education in the form of a "humanizing pedagogy." Oppressive, normative frames like racism, sexism, classism, nationalism, and so forth, limit our humanness.

Maria del Carmen Salazar (2013) writes, "Teachers who enact humanizing pedagogy engage in a quest for 'mutual humanization' with their students . . . where students are coinvestigators in dialogue with their teachers" (p. 127). For this to happen, teachers and students must make themselves vulnerable to one another. One of the principles underlying a humanizing pedagogy is mutual vulnerability. No genuine relationship, including the one between a teacher and her students, exists without mutual vulnerability. This is more than equals letting down their guard, and it is not the same as mutual disclosure. Kwenda (as cited in Keet et al., 2009) explains mutual vulnerability in the context of cultural injustice: "Some people are forced, by coercion or persuasion, to submit to the burdensome condition of suspending—or more permanently surrendering—what they naturally take for granted, and then begin to depend on what someone else takes for granted" instead (Keet et al., 2009, p. 110). For example, when nondominant learners must conform to norms and structures not their own (often those of White, middle-class teachers), when their own ways of framing experience, both mentally and linguistically, and their natural responses must be put on hold, they become subject to a form of cultural injustice. They are put in the position of shouldering the burden of adjusting to a world not made with them in mind—for example, transgender students and differentiated bathrooms, English language learners and a monolingual majority, students with weight problems in schools with small desks and chairs. Minorities experience the two frames of reference—their own and the dominant one. People in the dominant frame generally experience only their own. For those who must shoulder the burden of two (or more) frames, actions become inhibited and self-conscious. One's very self must be proscribed; forced to be constantly self-conscious, they are robbed of the ability to be freely and fully themselves. In other words, the burden of adjustment and vulnerability rests with those from nondominant groups. Mutual vulnerability, in contrast, "dictates that this responsibility, this burden, be shared." This requires teachers and others who hold power (including other students) to "open up and render their frames vulnerable" to inquiry and critique (Keet et al., 2009, p. 110).

This is necessarily risky work and calls into question the very identities of everyone involved. Moving consciously into someone else's sense-making, and suspending one's own in order to do so, can feel like abandoning one's very identity, even one's reality. It requires entering someone else's (non) sense, which can feel disorienting and scary. Equally scary is having some-one else perceive one's own frames as nonsense. It is not simple. What does it mean for a teacher of color, for example, who is both in a position of power and from a nondominant group, to commit to mutual vulnerability? What would it have meant for me, dominant in so many ways (White, American, teacher), and yet vulnerable in so many other ways (female, nonfluent in French and Wolof, feeling my way in a postcolonial culture) in Sénégal? I can't help but think that mutual awareness of these realities, which research calls "intersectionality," along with dialogue, are key.

Thus, presence involves a willingness not only to see one's learners, but also to be seen by them, including inquiring together into that which limits the realization of everyone's humanness—from social structures to curriculum to teaching practices. There are few professions where one is both so powerful and so vulnerable at the same time. Often teachers view their own vulnerability as a liability and seek to prevent any "bleeding" lest the sharks (their students or colleagues) attack. Asking for help, copping to not knowing the answer to a question, receiving low student test scores, are all perceived as weaknesses to be avoided rather than vulnerabilities to be explored.

Students respond when the "real person" of the teacher shows up—and they can smell a fake a mile away. I hasten to add that being vulnerable does not mean sharing one's personal problems with students or disclosing pri-vate details. It does mean putting oneself in the position of not knowing, in the position of a learner, as a partner in inquiry. It does mean bringing one's whole self, blind spots and all, to the table. It does mean asking explicitly about the water one swims in. Presence requires mutual vulnerability.

CHAPTER 3

The Permeable Nature of Self and World

I once asked author Patricia Carini about the impact of her childhood on her view of the world. She recounted for me growing up on the prairies of South Dakota and the impact of the land and those wide-open spaces on her perception of the world. I recall her saying that she once put her face to the ground, flush with it, and had the overwhelming knowledge that she and the world were the same, made of the same stuff, and she found that both incredibly comforting and awe inspiring. I recall being struck by this insight and the truth of it. This sense of permeability between self and world, it turns out, is central to my notion of presence and learning.

ORIGINS

In his book, *The Swerve*, Stephen Greenblatt (2011) recounts the history of the didactic poem, *De Rerum Natura* (On the Nature of Things), written by Roman poet and philosopher Lucretius, who lived and wrote in the 1st century B.C.E. The poem bases its teachings on the writing of Epicurus (341–270 B.C.E.), an ancient Greek philosopher who believed human beings suffered unnecessarily from fear of death and the anger and punishment of the gods. Based on the theory put forth by the "atomist" Democritus in 500 B.C.E. that the world was composed of "the atom, the void, and nothing else" (Greenblatt, 2011, p. 75), Epicurus argued that the gods were powerless, unreal, and not to be feared. They held no dominion over humans after death, because, once dead, we return to the material forms of our origins: All material aspects of the world are composed of atoms, and we are, as Greenblatt writes, "made of the same matter as the stars and the oceans and all things else" (p. 8). "When we look up at the night sky and . . . marvel at the numberless stars, we are not seeing the handiwork of the gods or a crystalline sphere. . . . We are seeing the same material world of which we are a part and from whose elements we are made" (pp. 5–6). In other words, we do not survive except as atoms, the stuff of the world, after death and so are beyond the reach of the gods.

This 2,500-year-old idea that "we are stardust," presaged discoveries in modern physics and cosmology that materially we are, in fact, literally the universe and the universe is us. Not only are we made of the same "stuff," and in flux, like the stuff of the world, we (the world and ourselves) change in response to one another—the boundaries between us are permeable. This is not merely a metaphor but a physical truth.

Interaction and Continuity

Dewey (1934) also wrote extensively about the permeable nature of the individual and the stuff of the world. He contended that all experience comprises two elements, interaction and continuity. Interaction is the "first great consideration":

> The first great consideration is that life goes on in an environment, not merely in it but because of it, through interaction with it. No creature lives merely under its skin; its subcutaneous organs are means of connection with what lies beyond its bodily frame, and to which, in order to live, it must adjust itself, by accommodation and defense but also by conquest. (p. 13)

The environment refers not only to the material world, but also to other conditions that interact with "personal needs, desires, purposes, and capacities to create the experience which is had" (Dewey, 1938, p. 44), for example, the classroom environment—classroom rules and routines, its culture of kindness or harsh discipline, high standards or laissez-faire. An experience, then, is not an experience unless it involves interaction between the self and another person, the material world, the natural world, an idea, or whatever constitutes the environment at hand. Through interaction, both people and the world they encounter are changed: "In an experience, things and events belonging to the world, physical and social, are transformed through the human context they enter, while the live creature is changed and developed through its intercourse with things previously external to it" (Dewey, 1934, p. 246). "At its height it signifies complete interpenetration of self and the world of objects and events" (Dewey, 1934, p. 19). People cannot be separated from the world they inhabit.

Philosopher of science David Hawkins (1974/2002) takes the idea of interaction further, contending that one cannot know a person except as we see them in commerce with the world:

> A human being is a localized physical body, but you can't see him as a person unless you see him in his working relationships with the world around him. The more you cut off these working relationships, the more you put him in a box, figuratively or literally, the more you diminish him. (p. 53)

All of this is to say that we are human in our interactions with, and shared creation of, the world. Teaching that is present to the learner as a human being needs to make room for this essential aspect of what it means to be human. The learner is present to the world and its effect upon him, while the teacher is present to both the learner's interactions and their effects, including their effect upon the teacher herself. It is the teacher's job to make these interactions possible.

To return to my proposition that teaching is a response to learning rather than its cause, Dewey would say that it could not be otherwise. The learner's primary interaction is with the world. The role of the teacher is to construct the environment in which that interaction can happen and then to respond in a way that allows the learner to move forward and outward.

Phenomenology

Phenomenology is the philosophical study of the structures of experience and consciousness, and has much to say about the idea of the permeable nature of self and world. Phenomenologist Merleau-Ponty wrote:

> In so far as, when I reflect on the essence of subjectivity, I find it bound up with that of the body and that of the world, this is because my existence as subjectivity is merely one with my existence as a body and with the existence of the world, and because the subject that I am, when taken concretely, is inseparable from this and this world. (as cited in Dreyfus & Wrathall, 2009, p. 408)

In other words, as a subject—a person in a body who exists in the world—I cannot think of myself as separate from the world. What if this were how we thought about the classroom? If what Dewey and Merleau-Ponty and Hawkins say is true, then what are the implications for the teacher as she creates a curriculum, sets up the classroom environment, formulates activities and tasks, or assesses knowledge? Further, what are the implications if she ignores the human need for interaction with the world? If the former humanizes, doesn't the latter dehumanize?

PERMEABILITY OF SELF AND WORLD ACROSS PROFESSIONS

In an effort to explore the permeable nature of the human–world phenomenon, Mark Wrathall, professor of philosophy at the University of California, Riverside, and his colleagues interviewed several "masters" in different fields. They created a movie (Canavesio & Ruspoli, 2010) that was spurred by their desire to understand better the craft of master teacher and MIT professor Hubert Dreyfus (1929–2017), author of the book *Being-in-the-World* (1991) (Wrathall, personal communication, February, 9, 2017). They filmed and interviewed several practitioners across various "worlds": a jazz musician, a New Orleans Creole cook, a master Japanese wood carver, a Spanish Flamenco guitarist, a speedboat racer, and a juggler. Each speaks to the commitment, passion, and authenticity of craft and the permeable nature of themselves and their craft.

Bass player Ryan Cross speaks of his bass as an extension of himself: "Being connected to my instrument is being connected to myself. I have to be in touch here [touching the neck of the instrument], so I have to be in touch with myself. Myself, meaning the instrument becomes you." Master carpenter Hiroki Sakaguchi says that as a carpenter he has a particular way of engaging with the world. "Carpentry," he says, "is in the body." He strokes the wood, gauges the sharpness of his tools, leans his body into the planer with finely tuned pressure. He has a feel for it. Wrathall elaborates, describing Heidegger's explanation of the nature of a hammer. If you want to know what a hammer is, you don't think about the properties of the hammer, you don't describe it, you don't explain it. "You pick it up and you start driving some nails." Only then will you have something meaningful to say. This intimacy between a master and his work blurs the distinction between the two. Leah Chase was a pioneering chef of Creole cuisine. One of her assistants said of her, "People think of recipes; she *is* the recipe."

Hubert Dreyfus, whose teaching this film sought to understand better, was a researcher in artificial intelligence. He noted that the primary difference between humans and robots in their interactions with the world is that human beings care. In contrast to robots, we are touched and moved by the world, and desire to make meaning of it. Being human is, in part, he says, about understanding which facts, among an infinite number of facts, are relevant, which facts matter. "The trouble with computers is that they don't give a damn," he says. While a machine might be able to follow one of Leah Chase's recipes, a machine cannot respond to the quality of the food, the heat of the day, the mood of a street crowd, appreciations of past improvisations. A machine doesn't care. It may be able to respond *as if* it cares—like some AI counseling apps—but fundamentally it is unaffected. As Chase puts it, "Sermons don't make a saint and recipes don't make a cook." The food, in the end, will lack the taste of love.

For Flamenco guitarist Manuel Molina, love is at the heart of his craft. "It's like a prayer," he says in Spanish, "a way of giving thanks to life." Dreyfus refers to mastery as "responsiveness to the richness and the calling in the world." "We," he notes, are not "inside of us." "I" is not what is inside of me. We/I is the interplay of inside and outside, self and other, self and world—if, in fact, "self" can be conceived of as separate or definable at all.

"What anyone who is very skilled in a domain [including teaching] knows is that being very skilled means responding not just in general terms to a situation, but responding very specifically to what the situation demands," Dreyfus continues. In many ways I hear Dreyfus's words as a definition of presence in teaching. Mastery is a response to the details of a situation, or what Mary Kennedy (2019) calls the "highly contingent nature of teaching" (p. 140). That is, the coming together of the particulars of a situation and the particulars of the body and mind of a person—the in-tune-ment—is always particular to the person and the situation.

AUTHENTICITY AND CONNECTION

There is a certain risk involved in this kind of improvisation, but masters take the risk, Dreyfus points out, because they care. "What distinguished the kind of risks we're interested in from just bravado, is that the risks are taken in the interests of what somebody is committed to, that they've defined themselves in terms of, what makes the meaningful differences in their lives" (Heidegger called it "running forward into death." Stepping into a classroom sometimes—often—can feel exactly like this, especially if you are a new teacher!) But the risk is yours, that is, your response, your unique combination of self and situation, and it requires a sort of radical openness. "What happens when you have this commitment to a particular something, . . . you hold yourself open to it completely. . . . When we're working at our best we are not detached from the situation that we find ourselves in. Rather we are open." We are, in a word, authentic.

Being authentic is not being "as if" but being in the situation and taking the risk of responding with one's whole self rather than with only an idea of what "should" be done. When you are not authentic, it looks like what Sean Kelly, chair of the philosophy department at Harvard, refers to as "the teenaged boy" phenomenon. Once a boy has landed a date, he then behaves with his date as he thinks guys-who-know do, thus taking his attention away from the date and the situation, and placing it entirely on himself, thereby, as anyone will tell you, blowing his chances. Dreyfus (Canavesio & Ruspoli, 2010) explained it this way:

> When we understand the connectedness between ourselves and others and the world, we finally understand mastery as a responsiveness to the richness and the calling in the world, [and] that the source of meaning in our lives, isn't in us, . . . it's in our way of being in the world. Being-in-the-world is a unified phenomenon. When people are at their best and most absorbed in doing a skillful thing, they lose themselves into their absorption . . . the distinction between the master and the world disappears.

In other words, the world and I are continuous. When we experience life this way, Dreyfus says, "we can re-experience what people call the sacred."

The fact of our inextricable connection to one another and the world is what makes teaching matter. We are human and humanized in our relationships with one another and the world. To create a humanizing classroom means creating spaces (both inside and outside) where we as teachers can create and see—be present to—those interactions. We need to be able to witness the becoming of our students and respond in ways that will extend those connections, and their humanness. Only when we create opportunities for connection with the world do our students come to care for what they are learning about, which matters profoundly to the future of democracy and our planet.

CHAPTER 4

Inquiry

In this chapter I look at the superior power of inquiry over instinct, or gut feelings. Presence has a kind of new-age aura that might suggest it is closer to intuition than to cognition. I do not believe this to be the case. I even have doubts about the presumed magical nature of intuition itself. Presence results from focused attention, both cognitive and affective. I explore the power of inquiry through the work of researchers in psychology ("thin-slicing" and heuristics) and medicine. I end with its relevance to teaching.

THIN-SLICING AND INQUIRY

Malcolm Gladwell, in his 2005 bestseller *Blink*, talks about the phenomenon of "thin-slicing." Thin-slicing, writes Gladwell, is "the ability of our unconscious to find patterns in situations and behavior based on very narrow slices of experience" (p. 23). He points to multiple disciplines where thin-slicing is employed by experts to predict outcomes and behaviors; for example, "court sense" in basketball, the "coup d'oeil" in battle (at-a-glance-ness), or bird watchers' sense of a bird's "giss" (essentials of movement), which allows birders to identify a bird with just a glimpse at its flight.

He speaks at length about the work of John Gottman, whose research looks closely at couples' interactions. Gottman reportedly can predict with 90% accuracy, after close analysis of just 15 minutes of videotape, whether a couple will stay together. Since the early 1980s Gottman and his wife, Julie S. Gottman, in their "Love Lab," have documented and analyzed the micro-expressions of everyday interactions in the faces and bodies of thousands of couples. Using micro-segments of a 15-minute exchange, each second is coded as one of 20 separate codes like disgust, sadness, defensiveness, or neutrality, drawn from the Gottmans' Specific Affect coding system. Looking closely for both positive and negative indications of connection and disconnection, Gottman's team was able to identify signs of what helped relationships to thrive and what killed them. Positive signs fell into three categories: "love maps" of a partner's inner world, small and frequent gestures of appreciation and respect, and bids for connection or responses to a partner's attempt to connect. Negative signs, which they dubbed the "Four Horsemen of the [Couple's] Apocalypse," included defensiveness, stonewalling, criticism, and (especially) contempt. These elements, coupled with objective measurements like heart rate, body temperature, and movement, allowed Gottman's researchers to be able to thin-slice what they observed and predict with startling accuracy whether a couple would stay together.

The categories, both positive and negative, were developed over thousands of hours of observation, categorization, and testing; categories were discerned over many years, not with immediate insight. No one, points out Gladwell, comes to thin-slicing as a virginal expert. It is only after thousands of hours of close attention that such discernment is developed. Intuition in the absence of experience, he notes, is useless. So-called woman's intuition, for example, comes from paying close attention over many years to what matters to her about relationships. The eyes-behind-the-head of a teacher or a parent are based on years of being on the qui vive for certain behaviors that have become deeply familiar.

HEURISTICS AND INQUIRY

While Gladwell cites research that affirms the power of observation and underscores the notion that intuition is more likely to be the result of someone having processed vast amounts of information than of someone getting "hits" out of nowhere, psychologists Daniel Kahneman and Amos Tversky's work points to how flawed our decisionmaking processes can be, especially those based on "gut feelings" or what might feel like thin-slicing. Their work highlights our tendency to fit our experiences into the narratives we create of our own lives and the lives of others. Their years of research, for which they received the 2002 Nobel Prize in economics, demonstrated that, as human beings, we defer to the easiest and most plausible explanation for what we see. More precisely, we use "heuristics," which provide a rule of thumb, or shortcut, to a decision that fits a familiar pattern or narrative, and "feels right." These decisions frequently are based on stories that we tell ourselves that reinforce beliefs that we already hold. Kahneman (2011) writes:

> It is the consistency of the information that matters for a good story, not its completeness. Indeed, you will often find that knowing little makes it easier to fit everything you know into a coherent pattern. . . . The confidence that individuals have in their beliefs depends mostly on the quality of the story they can tell about what they see, even if they see little. We often fail to allow for the possibility that evidence that should be critical to our judgment is missing—what we see is all there is. (p. 87)

Kahneman (2011) has identified two perceptive "systems"—System 1 and System 2. System 1 is fast and automatic, requiring little or no mental effort. System 2, on the other hand, is "deliberate, effortful, and orderly"—that is, careful and slow. But is it also lazy—it doesn't like to work if it doesn't have to. So it looks for shortcuts—heuristics—to lighten the cognitive load. It likes to defer to System 1. System 2 is "more of an apologist for the emotions of System 1 than a critic of those emotions" (p. 104) and has no trouble rationalizing the decisions taken by System 1.

Kahneman has even named this tendency—the What You See Is All There Is (WYSIATI) principle. If we perceive only a little, which is easier to do if we are alone, or in a hurry, or, as Kahneman points out, lazy, we come to conclusions that fit that limited body of evidence, without doing the harder work of searching for more or disconfirming evidence. For example, when my son was in 3rd grade he, like many 8-year-old boys, was active, curious, joyful, and a little clumsy. One day he knocked a jar of red paint over and it spilled onto a classmate's sweatshirt. His teacher, Ms. C., clearly fed up, grabbed him around the waist and planted him in front of the sink. ("I felt like a piece of paper, Mama," he later told me.) That night I received a phone call from Ms. C. suggesting that Jon's "pattern of hyperactivity" needed to "be looked at." When I pushed her to say what "needed to be looked at" meant, it became clear to me that it was code for "he has ADHD—attention deficit hyperactivity disorder; maybe he should be medicated." I asked her directly if this was indeed what she meant. She then backed down and that was the end of it. Still, she clearly had a notion of what a pattern of "active" behavior denoted and she created a story wherein Jon's behavior fit that pattern. What she had not taken into account, from Kahneman's perspective, was this: While all ADHD 3rd-grade boys may be active, not all active 3rd-grade boys have ADHD.

The most common heuristic device is story. Stories help to order the messiness of the world. As soon as we can find a coherent story to make sense of what we see, we stick with it, with unwarranted confidence, making other evidence fit within those parameters or, if it doesn't fit, dismissing the evidence altogether. As Dewey knew, recognition is easier than perception. Ms. C.'s story was simple. Frustrated by Jon, the narrative of ADHD gave her reason both to relieve herself of any responsibility and to put "the problem" into others' hands.

How does Kahneman recommend countering the flaws in System 1 and strengthening System 2? After all, he points out, questioning your gut feelings, especially in the face of a situation requiring a rapid response, is uncomfortable. He suggests building in structural supports. Organizations like schools, or groups, can build in such structures, both linguistic and procedural, to remind individuals to stop and think. (The reflective process outlined in Part IV is one such structural support.)

Below I look at healthcare, a service profession that, like education, is particularly vulnerable to heuristics. Again drawing on personal experience, I tell a story about a diagnosis that, if the diagnostic process had been slowed down and there had been inquiry into initial conclusions, might have led to a different outcome.

MEDICINE AND INQUIRY

In March 2013 I got a phone call from my brother saying that our vital 83-year-old mother was flying home from her vacation early. A former high school Spanish teacher, she was in Oaxaca, Mexico, where she had spent 3 weeks living with a Mexican family, boning up on her Spanish through daily practice and lessons. My brother told me he would be picking Mom up at the airport the next day. Apparently she was in great pain, particularly in her hands, shoulders, and wrists. We were told that she had been climbing a pyramid in nearby Monte Alban 2 days before and the next day she was crippled by the pain in her joints.

The next day, back home, we arranged a visit to Mom's doctor. He recommended that she see an orthopedist. X-rays apparently revealed bone on bone arthritis in her right shoulder and what might be a torn rotator cuff. She was scheduled for shoulder replacement surgery in early May.

In the meantime, however, she continued to have pain in her knees, ankles, and hands, each of which periodically would show signs of significant swelling. Her spirits were low, and she was scared of what was happening to her body. I think she was scared she was dying. I repeatedly visited her in the intervening weeks, and my brother kept a constant eye on her. He frequently referred to other signs of discomfort: hoarseness and a persistent cough, difficulty hearing, fatigue, and a loss of appetite. This vital woman, who up until March was so alive and active—travel, book clubs, museum work, long walks, and two "boyfriends," both of whom wanted to marry her—had suddenly, seemingly, grown old.

I was baffled by the migrating swelling in her hands, knees, and legs—the long, beautiful legs of a champion tennis player and ski instructor—and kept raising it with her doctors. "She has arthritis," said the orthopedist. The arthritis in her shoulder was evidence of that. Other doctors chalked the deafness, hoarseness, and fatigue up to "getting old."

In May, before Mom was wheeled into the operating room for the scheduled shoulder replacement, I asked the surgeon, again, "What about that swelling in her legs? It's not normal." I don't remember her exact response, but the gist was, "Not my department." As the summer rolled on, despite physical and occupational therapy, warmer weather, and walks, Mom got worse. Her energy flagged, and all of her other symptoms worsened as well. Finally, in late August I got another call from my brother. Mom was in the hospital with what doctors thought was congestive heart failure.

I hurried to the hospital that afternoon. As I entered her room, she turned to me and, through tears, in a voice no bigger than a dust mote, said, "I want to die." The next 4 days in the hospital were spent trying to figure out what was going on. She had a team of specialists: a cardiologist, a pulmonologist, a hematologist, a rheumatologist, and an internist, or "hospitalist." It was like the blind men and the elephant, each seeing her through his or her own specialized lens, except the elephant was my diminished mother. Finally, on the 4th day, after the congestive heart failure diagnosis had been rejected, along with pneumonia, a young pulmonologist, who had replaced the first one (as the entire first team rotated out), came in to see Mom. Again, I mentioned the swelling—I also asked the doctor whether she would like to hear my mother's story. "Yes," she said sitting down on the edge of Mom's bed, "Please," and gestured for me to begin. I recounted the story of my mother before she got ill and walked the doctor through the past 6 months of symptoms. The doctor was present, silent but attentive to whatever the narrative revealed, but, I imagine, also mentally testing her theories of what the evidence might point to as she listened. When I'd finally finished, all the facts laid out like a collection of short stories, the doctor said, "I think I may know what is happening. But I need to do one test."

My champion mother, who was in such pain, agreed to submit herself to one more test, but only after my sister and I made a deal with her. If the doctor's plan didn't work we would take her to hospice, where she had wanted to go from the beginning. "Let's hit one more shot over the net!" she said, gamely. And the test revealed definitive results: Wegener's disease, or granulomatosis with polyangiitis, a rare autoimmune condition resulting in the leakage of small blood vessels into the joints, lungs, and sinuses, and finally the internal organs.

While the diagnosis was correct, the drugs, Cytoxan and prednisone, were too little, too late. Per our deal with her, 7 days after she went into the hospital we took Mom to hospice, where she died 48 hours later.

I appreciate the uncertain nature of medical care and the real difficulty of diagnosing a rare disease that manifests with common symptoms of aging. I even question whether Mom would have chosen to take the strong chemo drugs that might have kept her alive longer, had she been diagnosed earlier. Nonetheless I regret, deeply, that she lived in such pain thinking that she was the problem. That if she'd only worked harder, she would have gotten better and felt less sick. I regret deeply that we didn't have a name for what she had so that she could have worked with a palliative care doctor and managed the pain, and died in a dignified way over which she had some control. I also regret that I was not more aggressive in seeking answers instead of being so accepting of earlier diagnoses. I knew the swelling was not merely arthritis and I deferred where I should have inquired.

The work of Dr. Rita Charon in narrative medicine and Dr. Jerome Groopman, in his 2007 book *How Doctors Think*, address two aspects of my mother's story. Charon, an MD/PhD at Columbia University Medical School, is the founder and director of the narrative medicine program there. Narrative medicine, she writes, "attempts to illuminate the universally true by revealing the particular." This stands in contrast to a logicoscientific approach, which "attempts to illuminate the universally true by transcending the particular" (Charon, 2001, p. 1898). Charon sees the space between the doctor and the patient as a "third space" between a reader and a text where "multiple sources of local—and possibly contradicting—authority replace master authorities; instead of being monolithic and hierarchically given, meaning is apprehended collaboratively, by the reader and the writer, the observer and the observed, the physician and the patient, [the teacher and the student]" (p. 1898). That is, the doctor is not the sole authority in the room. The patient, the family, the nurses are all sources of valuable information. While I spoke on my mother's behalf, it was her story I was telling; the pulmonologist did the inquiring and then the close reading of the particulars. Together, she, my mother, my siblings, and I decided how to move forward.

Groopman (2007) notes that doctors do not like "not knowing." Like the rest of us, they use heuristics to figure out efficiently what might be going on. Once they find evidence that confirms the story they have constructed (e.g., "She's 84. She's just getting old. She's got arthritis."), they tend to look for the evidence that confirms that story. They tend to stop at recognition rather than persist in perception. As Groopman says:

> Physicians tend to go with their first impressions. The initial biases in a physician's thinking are often reinforced by his selective survey of diagnostic data. We all are inclined to seize on an apparently positive finding and ignore what may be negative and contradictory. (p. 262)

To counter this tendency, Groopman recommends embracing doubt and intentionally inserting it into the diagnostic process. Not a crippling doubt, but a cautious doubt—where could I be wrong? Where could the experts be wrong? What am I not seeing? Where else might the evidence point? Misdiagnosis is, says Groopman, the elephant in the doctor's room. The kind of suspension of certainty with an openness to further inquiry and investigation that Groopman speaks of, and my mother's pulmonologist practiced, results, ideally, in discernment, premised on acts of perception and inquiry. This is clearly hard when everyone is pressing for an answer and time is of the essence. The same thing could be said about the classroom.

TEACHING, INQUIRY, AND PRESENCE

Although the above is a medical story, its parallel in teaching should be obvious. While we may not deal in literal life and death, we can have a life-giving or a deadening impact on students. We can humanize or dehumanize. Staying open, disciplining the urge to diagnose, requires a stance of humble "not knowing." I want to explore this, along with the importance of a sustained and sustaining wonder and curiosity about the human condition.

For a teacher, or anyone in a position of authority, to embrace not knowing seems counterintuitive. Aren't we in that position because we know? Don't learners come to teachers in order to "get" what teachers know? Isn't it our job to "transfer" and "impart" knowledge?

It is, I believe, our job to know our subject, and to always be making new and more complex connections. The objective of that knowing is not to show everyone how much we know but to open doors and windows through which others can step so that they might make their own connections. This takes enormous preparation. As I said earlier, such preparation is key to a capacity for presence. As Dewey (1933) said, "Unless the teacher's mind has mastered the subject matter in advance, unless it is thoroughly at home in it, using it unconsciously without need of express thought, he will not be free to give full time and attention to observation and interpretation of the pupils' intellectual reactions" (p. 270).

What a teacher cannot know ahead of time is what will happen in that space between learner and content, between a person and the world. That is what a teacher is present to, the space where her attention, curiosity, and inquiry live. A classroom of 25 6-year-olds presents a daunting contextual complexity. A teacher has to figure out not only what a student is doing and thinking, but also what the other 24 students are doing and thinking; she also must keep order and deal with a level of 6-year-old language that requires constant translation. Inquiry is, therefore, constant and ongoing.

The following classroom example comes from a brief encounter between Maddy, a kindergarten teacher, and a small group of learners. Maddy is teaching a lesson using plastic coins—pennies, nickels, dimes, and quarters—focusing on the difference between number (one nickel) and value (five cents). She keeps a sharp eye on the six students (as well as on the other 15 who are working independently and with aides). She keeps posing problems that ask her students to use the knowledge they have to figure out what they don't yet know. "How much is this?" she asks ("much" implying value rather than number), sliding one nickel in front of each of them. "One!" "Five!" they call out. To resolve the apparent conflict Maddy takes away Michael's nickel and asks how many pennies she should give him in exchange. "Five pennies!" (At this point, Christopher, who is lost, leans over to me and whispers in my ear, "I love you." Maddy smiles. She is also present to these moments.) She slides Christopher three nickels and asks, "How much?" "Three!" "What else?" Some students know immediately that it's 15 cents, and she gives them harder problems.

Then Maddy returns her attention to Christopher and asks, "How much is a nickel?" "Five cents!" She shoves him a pile of pennies and Christopher independently counts three small groups of five pennies each, and then counts by ones to 15. Maddy continues to work with the students, shifting the game from the exchange of coins to buying items at a store. "What would you like?" "An ice cream!" "That will be 35 cents." Yasmin counts out a quarter, and two nickels. And so on. The presence that is required for this work, the constant process of inquiry–observation–response, is deceptively simple. In reality, it requires a deep level of expertise and in-tune-ment with the students, with the subject matter, and with oneself. As educator Ted Swartz (1978) once put it:

> Once it is clear that learning is an internal, purposeful activity under the control of the learner, [a teacher's] efforts towards enhancing that activity become unavoidably saturated with a concern for knowing as clearly as possible and at every moment how the learning is (or is not) taking place. One's capacity for constructive intervention is directly dependent on one's clarity of perception into the shifting currents of inner movements of the learner. The tool for that perception is one's self, as that self is attendant to the effects on oneself of the inputs generated by what the learner is doing. (p. 5)

What Swartz is saying here is profound. Once a teacher realizes that learning can't be stuck onto someone like so many Post-its, but can happen only under the power of the learner, it becomes incumbent upon the teacher to concern herself with knowing as clearly as possible whether and how that learning is happening. Only when we see learning, can we effectively respond with what is needed next. The teacher's self is the instrument of perception that "reads" that learning. I would add that the instrument of the self can get very cluttered with the filters of the self as well. The various judgments and stories (heuristics) we carry of individual learners, types of learners, race, class, gender, and various "-isms" from ADHD to second-language learners, shape our responses unless we are onto them. At the same time that the teacher is inquiring into the child's understanding, she also needs to turn that inquiring lens on herself.

A second form of inquiry in the classroom, in addition to the ongoing inquiry described above, is reflective in nature. After teaching for about 20 minutes, Maddy stops to reflect with her students on their experience with the coins. She asks what might still be confusing to them. Michael, who had seemed so sure of his knowledge, said, "I don't know how much a nickel is on the other side." Maddy looks puzzled. "Can you say more?" "How much is a nickel when it's tails?" he asks. Maddy, taking a not-knowing stance (what Cochran-Smith and Lytle, 2009, call an inquiry stance), is able to see that Michael's understanding of the value of a coin did not apply to the whole coin, only the heads side! Once this is clear, she is able to respond, saying that it's the same value, no matter which side is showing. She tests his understanding by experimenting with a few other coins and is satisfied. But if she had assumed he knew, instead of inquiring, she could have left him with his misconception.

When I shared this story with another teacher, she told me she would have asked Michael, "Is it still a nickel when I turn it over?" But her question comes from a place of knowing and wanting him to know what she knew, rather than of inquiry and wondering about the sense that Michael was making. She would be listening for her answer rather than his. Even with the "correct answer"—it's still a nickel—it could have still left him wondering.

Presence requires inquiry and a stance of not knowing as well as a deep knowledge of all the different directions that a subject, or an illness, or any journey might take. As a lactation nurse whom I know once said of the teaching she does with new mothers, "Teaching is like traveling, only the culture comes to you, and you become the learner." Presence requires a deep familiarity with the territory in question, but also a deep respect for that unknown territory that is the experience of the learner, patient, or traveler.

CHAPTER 5

Love

Love is an awfully big subject—one that no sane person writing a book about teaching would touch. Philosopher of science David Hawkins (1974/2002), who wrote much about teaching that has influenced my own views, once said, "I think the attitude of love, which is the parental attitude, isn't really the appropriate one. Perhaps the word 'respect' might be more appropriate" (p. 53). While I would agree that respect is essential in teaching and certainly to a stance of presence, I respectfully disagree that there is no place for love. In fact, I believe it is essential to presence. I can honestly say, and have said directly to them, that I love my students.

LOVE AND TRUSTING THE LEARNER WITHIN

Let me say, I do not necessarily like all my students, although it is rare that I don't. But it is not hard for me to love the learner in each one of them. What I see, and love, in each student is the learner within, that part of them that has figured out (and continues to) so much about how to survive in the world. They have taught themselves to talk, to stand, to walk, to run, to read, to write, to tell funny stories, to whistle, to offer comfort, to persist, to build block castles, to read facial expressions. The list is endless, and they have learned these things largely on their own. Entirely on their own, in fact, since no one can learn for someone else. When they started as learners at birth or maybe before, they were new, naked, vulnerable, and yet so powerful in their capacity to figure out the world, that they immediately put themselves to work. I am in awe. It is this part of them that I truly, absolutely, unconditionally love and trust. I trust their capacity to learn. It is this aspect of their otherwise tricky selves that I have no problem opening myself wide to.

Hubert Dreyfus spoke of authenticity. I can think of nothing more authentic than this love. Admittedly, I sometimes have to remind myself to push past the less lovable aspects of my learners (and myself—the Pool Bitch still shows up) but I do it because I know, with conviction, what lies beneath. I try to listen, to be there, because that wide-open learner might emerge at any moment to delight me and leave me in awe.

LOVE AND THE MORAL DIMENSION OF PRESENCE

David Hansen (2004) uses the concept of "moral perception." He captures the emotional quality of being touched and moved by children and what he refers to as "the good." "Serious-minded teachers are moved or quickened to action by the good and by expressions of the good. . . . Integral to this quality of moral perception is the disposition of being attracted, metaphorically speaking, to the good of one's students, colleagues, school, and community" (p. 134). Such a teacher "expresses a philosophy that looks to the next moment in a spirit of hopeful anticipation, as if the next moment were that which, metaphorically speaking, gives birth to whomever and whatever persons might become" (p. 141). He also hints at what many teachers are drawn to when they choose to teach: making a difference in the world and doing work that is bigger than themselves—meaningful work that adds value to the world. I think this speaks to love.

How is this love realized in concrete terms? Hansen speaks of preparing a "dwelling place," a place of welcome, where a person might do more than merely hang his hat. The space is both physical and relational. To prepare a physical space for learning, "a clean, well-lighted space"[3] where there is room for everyone, is an act of hospitality.

LOVE AND LISTENING

A space where everyone is welcome is a space where everyone is listened to with respect and interest. This is most evident to me with my students for whom English is a second or third (or fourth!) language. Frequently students from outside the United States arrive with unpracticed English and limited cultural knowledge that delimits their full participation in class. I require participation in small- and large-group discussion, which forces these students, many of whom come from cultures where good students listen to teachers rather than being listened to by them, to go way outside their comfort zone. It can be discomfiting for both those students and the other students who must watch them struggle. In an attempt to protect the non-native student, fellow students often will nod as though understanding, even if they don't have a clue what the student has just said. Because they don't want to put the student on the spot or cause embarrassment, they smile, murmur a polite, noncommittal "Unh," and then carry on where the conversation left off, without the contribution of the non-native speaker having made any visible impact.

The metaphor I use for this experience is this: Have you ever thrown a pebble down a well and listened for the sound it will make when it hits the water? Well, throwing the pebble of one's thoughts down a well and never hearing that satisfying *ploop!* as it makes contact can leave the speaker feeling disconcerted and disconnected. It both cuts others off from the internal workings and essences of that student, and cuts that student off from their own sense-making, their very humanness, as imperfect as it may be.

To counter this lacuna, I risk saying to my students, "I'm not sure I quite understand what you're saying. Can you say it again?" Or, "Can you give me an example?" Or, "Can you show me where in the text you see that?" Rather than protecting them, enclosing them in a protective casing, I want to know them. So I push them, gently, because I believe they will have something interesting to say. I also do this with my native speakers, who will say things in perfectly good English, but not always with clarity. I want to know what they are saying rather than assuming their thoughts are fully formed (and match mine), or suggesting that they have nothing of value to contribute, or that I think they are fragile. My students have told me how much this means to them, that I stay with them until they—we—have uncovered what they mean to say. In other words, I try to be present not only to who they are, but also to who they are becoming in the process.

LOVE AND ATTENTION TO WHAT CANNOT BE SEEN

To be present to students is to be present to so much that can't be seen. Immigrant students in K–12 settings, some of them students with limited or interrupted formal education, often arrive with violent histories scarred by trauma. Others come from traumatic home situations, poverty, or neglect, or simply have had a bad day or are feeling lost. One 5th-grade student, Bettina, from a school in the Bronx recently explained to me the pain inherent in being "behind":

> Sometimes [kids] just can't find a way to succeed, to follow the expectations, because some kids are just all the way up here [her hand gestures at an invisible line above her head], and you're just at the bottom. And you just want to find a person that you can relate to, but you can't find the person so then you just start like, being that class clown, you just start going low. But seriously, you just really need a person to help you.

Creating a clean and well-lit space for the telling of these experiences and bearing witness to their telling is, I contend, an act of love.

Along with a welcoming physical space, one creates a metaphorical space for others in part by preparing oneself. Joseph Goldstein (2013) implies that we create a compassionate space through the emptying of self. "Compassion," he writes, "is the very activity of emptiness of self. This is compassion not as a stance of the ego or even as a particular practice, but as the spontaneous expression of a heart and mind free of self-reference" (p. 367). He refers to a monk who expressed his love for humanity as the desire to throw open his monk's robes wide enough to "gather up all the people in this floating world" (p. 94). Many teachers recognize this feeling and the desire to gather up all their students' learner selves into their "robes."

LOVE OF SUBJECT MATTER

It is worth noting here that love is not merely between a teacher and her students. An important aspect of love, when it comes to presence in teaching, is love of one's subject matter and of the world itself. Such a love means a passion for both one's subject and how it connects to other subject matter, that is, the rest of life. As an example, I have, for many years, worked with students to understand the movements of the moon, sun, and earth relative to one another—sunrise and sunset, day and night, the seasons, moonrise and moonset, the phases of the moon, the mechanics of eclipses, and the significance of latitude and longitude, as well as "where we are" in space.

I see these elements not as isolated pieces of information to memorize but rather as aspects of everyday life and experience that it matters to know about. Why does it matter? Because I want to know where I am in the universe, and how this fragile blue planet, made of what I am made of, works. To know something deeply is to come to care about it. To know my physical location in the solar system gives me a sense of the miracle as well as the insignificance of our existence. To know how its bodies move in relationship to one another engenders wonder and excitement at being able to predict where the moon will be on a given day. To see magnificence in the everyday phenomena of light, night, a silvery sliver of moon, and the change of seasons gives me great joy. By now this knowledge is deeply a part of me, and I love opening these doors to others, as my teacher (Eleanor Duckworth) did for me.[4]

Lewis Hyde, in his book *The Gift* (1983), wrote that part of receiving a true gift is the desire to give what you have received away to others, to share it. I recall my deep desire to share what I had learned about the moon with my husband, and later with my children and extended family. It wasn't so much a desire to display my knowledge as it was to bring them into this expanded world that I now inhabited and to share my discovery, which was too beautiful to keep to myself. As one of my classmates put it, "To learn about [the moon] satisfied my curiosity; to tell it to someone else satisfied my soul."

The shadow side of loving our subject is the desire to have others love it as we do, and understand it as we do. The challenge is to be present to their making sense of it, to their own wonderful ideas (Duckworth, 1987), and to follow them rather than getting them to follow us. Perhaps this is another way of emptying the self and loving the learner. This is as true for fellow learners who have already worked out their understanding as it is for teachers. It is a sacrifice, this withholding, because the desire to share wonderful ideas is so strong. It is much easier to "bestow" knowledge than to organize a structure for others to discover it. The former leaves the learners fully accountable for remembering what the teacher has said, and it leaves them alone in the remembering. But when the learning happens in dialogue, in the process of actively uncovering knowledge, it is shared, worked, and internalized in the process.

LOVE AND SELF-COMPASSION

A final aspect of the role of love in presence is self-compassion. Teaching is perhaps the most widely judged, blamed, and second-guessed profession in the world. As sociologist Dan Lortie (1975) pointed out, teachers are "special but shadowed." They are both honored and looked down upon as "just teachers," praised for their dedicated work and scorned for doing work "anyone" could do, all with long, "unearned" vacations. They are judged for having unions that demand more money and better working conditions, yet exhorted to be more professional. In short, society's "professed regard" for teachers and its "real regard" have never truly aligned.

Teachers are further held responsible for students' test scores, even though studies show that test results are a more complex story than a simple cause (teaching) and effect (test scores) framework would suggest. Learning depends on many things, from students' willingness to learn, to the social surround that supports teaching and learning, to good teaching, which is distinct from successful teaching. The former denotes skill and care; the latter, student achievement (Fenstermacher & Richardson, 2005). And yet the public persists in seeing a straight line between teaching and test scores that holds teachers accountable for factors over which they have little control.

Not long ago, I sat in a room with three experienced teachers all in tears, as they described the pressures of trying to live up to such expectations. While I believe these expectations by society need adjusting, in the meantime a little self-compassion and acceptance are in order. It goes without saying that being present to one's own needs, being compassionate with oneself, is necessary if we are going to be present and loving toward others, especially a roomful of demanding children, hallways of middle school students with unharnessed hormones, or collections of sleep-deprived high school students whose worlds are crammed and compartmentalized to a mind-numbing, often exhausting degree.

CONCLUSION

I have explored my understanding of presence as a condition of wide-awakeness and mindfulness, and as an outgrowth of Dewey's philosophy. I have further explored five elements of presence I believe to be essential.

Presence requires attitudes of open-mindedness, directness, wholeheart-edness, responsibility, curiosity, and equanimity; mutual vulnerability; an awareness of the permeable nature of self and world; a stance of inquiry; and an openness to love. These elements are not exclusive of one another, and there are clear overlaps among them. Nor are they exhaustive. To be present is to learn, to be changed, to be affected, to be moved, to respond with compassion and deep knowledge of self, other, subject matter, and the various contexts that surround all of these. I now move to these elements of self, other, subject matter, and context—that to which one is present.

Part III

WHAT WE ARE PRESENT TO:
I, THOU, IT, AND CONTEXT

The purpose of Part III is to identify what there is for a teacher to be present to and to provide language with which to talk about it—both the parts and the dynamics of practice. Having words for these elements makes talking about them easier.

The I, Thou, It, and Context framework is a bit like the grid that a painter puts over a scene to be able to see each piece without being overwhelmed by the whole. In reflecting on teaching, it is also useful to be able to ask about these elements as a way of inquiring into all aspects of teaching rather than a select one or two, or to know how a select one or two fit into the whole picture of teaching. For example, if one is having problems with a student, it is useful to look not only at the student, but at that student's interactions with other students and adults; the student's race, class, and gender; the subject matter and how it is organized; the classroom set-up, and so forth. In this chapter I literally map out the elements in play, describing them each individually and then in interaction with one another.

To the layperson, teaching can look easy. Most people, by the time they leave school, have observed and participated in well over 10,000 hours of it firsthand, as students. After all this passive absorption, we think we know a lot about teaching. Unsurprisingly, teachers tend to teach the way they were taught[1] and we all have an opinion about it. School boards are generally made up of noneducators. How hard could it be . . . ?

Hard, as it turns out. It is not a simple, I-teach-you-learn formula. It is, as educational historian Larry Cuban (2013), says, complex. Cuban makes a helpful distinction between complex and complicated systems. Brain surgery and rocket science, he writes, are *complicated*. Confidence in performance along with predictable and carefully monitored results are the air that brain surgeons and rocket scientists breathe. Classrooms, on the other hand, are *complex* systems, "constantly buffeted by unpredictable events and interrelated factors over which participants have no control" (p. 156). They are composed of curricula, teachers and students, their actions, interactions, and invisible cognitive and emotional inner actions. In addition, there are contextual forces at play. Each person is shaped by external forces—social class, gender, sexual orientation, the legacies of slavery, immigration, histories of oppression, trauma, and loss—all of which, and many, many more, from the microlevel of the classroom or family to the macrolevels of war or national policy, determine the contours, both psychological and physical, of the classroom.

How can one possibly be present to all that? (And I've just touched the surface here.) Who has the time or bandwidth? A teacher must balance priorities. There is learning, there is coverage, there are test scores and "adequate yearly progress," not to mention annual professional performance reviews. Coverage—getting through the curriculum—often drives the train because this is the basis on which teachers are judged. Or rather, teachers race to cover everything that might be on the state tests, because they are judged on the basis of those results. "Any questions?[2] No? Good. (Because we don't have that kind of time.) Let's move on." Many teachers know this is not the way to teach and they feel the pull of authentic learning acutely. But they also feel compelled not to let their students, their principals, their school, and community, all of which also are judged on test results, down. And yet, ironically, attention to who students are, the internal workings of the self, the complexities of subject matter, context, and their interactions is essential to students' success.

CHAPTER 6

The Teaching Triangle

Its Parts

In 1967 philosopher of science and education David Hawkins published his essay, "I, Thou, and It," which focused on the relationship between the teacher (I) and her students (Thou), and the central role of subject matter (It) (see Figure 6.1). Any "It," he wrote, is merely a piece of the *"great It"* (emphasis in original), that is, the world from which the It is excerpted. Hawkins did not touch upon context except as the "great It"—the world— subsumes context. However, it is a dimension that merits as much reflection as any of the other dimensions.

Much has been written about the nodes of this triangle and the contexts in which each sits (Ball & Forzani, 2007); for example, the lives of

Figure 6.1. The I, Thou, It, and Contexts

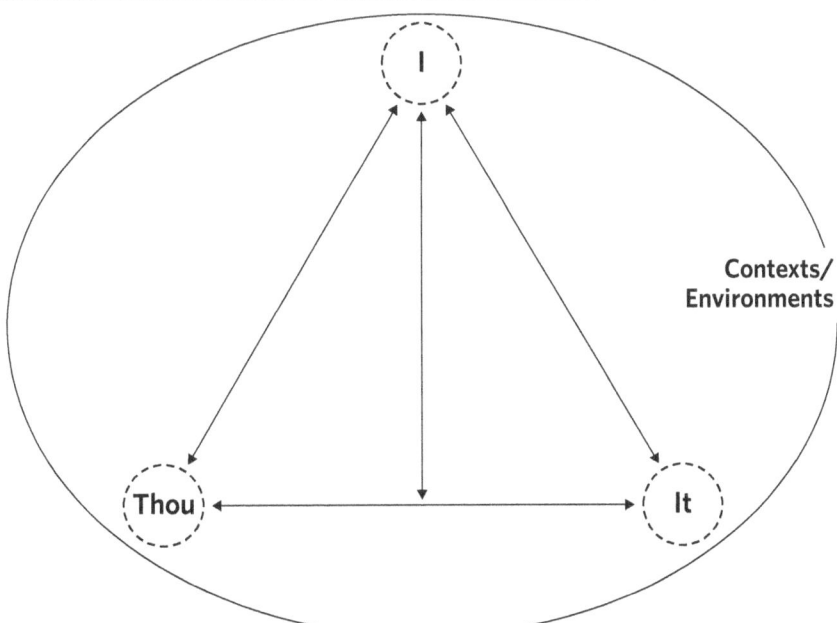

teachers, curriculum, and student performance. Less, however, has been written about what happens in their dynamic relationships (those two-directional arrows in the diagram). As Ball and Forzani write, "Knowing about and understanding teachers, learners, content, or environments—or even knowing and understanding all of these entities—is not a substitute for knowing about and understanding *the dynamic relationships among them that constitute the core of the educational process*" (p. 531, emphasis added). Teachers, and students themselves, are often the ones best situated to observe these dynamics. Conversations about them are seldom had in the classroom, although when they are, they can indeed be rich and productive. More often, conversations happen in the teachers' room, where they are less productive than they might be.

THE I (TEACHER)

At the top of the triangle is the "I," the teacher. I sometimes have seen the I placed at the bottom of the triangle, on a parallel with the Thou (learner). I understand and agree with the suggestion of equality therein, but I also think that positioning the teacher where she can oversee the interaction between the Thou and the It makes sense. She has a different job from the learner's. Although the role of the teacher is singular, there are multiple dimensions to it, as will become evident.

The Teacher Community

Although teachers are often the only adult in the room and may go for years without any other adult seeing them teach, they are, in fact, accompanied by other "I's," other teachers and colleagues, both present and absent. Most obviously, they are surrounded by other teachers in their school, or even in their classroom—associate teachers, aides, coaches, mentors, professional development staff, principals. They also are accompanied by more peripheral colleagues—social workers, guidance counselors, school psychologists. Less physically present, but still vital, are more distant colleagues who represent the field—researchers, writers of fiction and nonfiction, poets, philosophers, bloggers, journalists, and public intellectuals. Taken together, these represent a community of I's.

The more teachers are aware of and draw upon these resources, the richer their practice. In my work with beginning teachers, I am often aware of their assumption that, if they are "good" teachers, they will not need to ask for help from other teachers. They assume that after a year and a half of teacher education, they should know "it all." This view is reinforced by the public, which bemoans the inability of teacher education to produce "quality teachers," not understanding the complexity of what must be attended and responded to in the classroom. But teachers can draw strength and ideas from their professional communities—those provided or those they make themselves. My own teaching has been greatly enriched by these colleagues, both actual and virtual, and I cannot imagine teaching without them.

I as Learner

The I's primary role is as teacher but also, importantly, the I is a learner. In fact, a learning stance sits at the very heart of presence. Teachers are learners of their subject matter, their students, and their own selves, as well as the various contexts in which these all exist (see Figure 6.2). As a constant learner, the teacher needs to be free to observe and interact skillfully with the other nodes. I will say more about this when I look at the interactions between the I and the Thou and It.

Inner Actions

Every time teachers walk into the classroom, they carry their selves with them. Wherever you go, as the saying goes, there you are. Teachers bring along their beliefs about teaching and learning and the world, certain attitudes like generosity, patience, trust, and so forth (and, of course, their opposites), lofty beliefs and aspirations, passions, and fears—all the lenses through which they see themselves, their role, their students, and the world.

Figure 6.2. The I

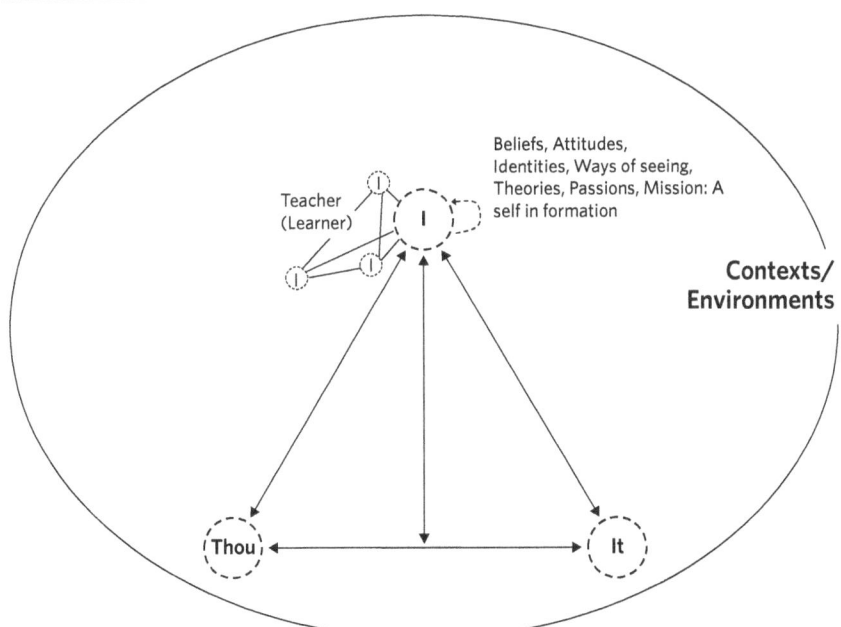

These are all aspects that also are constantly in flux and in the process of being refined, discarded, and amended.

The degree to which teachers are aware of the existence and influence of these inner actions—self-awareness—represents the degree to which they can, in terms of the mindfulness literature, engage in "right action"—acting with compassion and with a mind to students' best next steps rather than as, say, the Pool Bitch.

In a recent class with my doctoral students I was reminded of how easy it is to slip into the cloak of one's assumptions. We were discussing school structures, particularly in light of critical pedagogy, having just read a chapter from Joe Kincheloe's (2008) book by the same name. Alert to my past experiences where students claimed color blindness and assumed level playing fields or thought in terms of pulling oneself up by one's own bootstraps, I was already listening to their contributions with my own judgmental slant.

One student, whom I'll call Helen, offered that "low-income schools" should maybe have individualized educational programs (IEPs) the way students do. What I heard through my own filters was that inner-city (read: Black and Brown) schools are not as smart as the rest of us. On the alert for such comments, I jumped in with a warning to be careful with how she was casting a whole slice of society. From there, many others in the class, some with experience in minority schools, piled on, leaving poor Helen defending her earlier comments and repeatedly trying to explain what she had been trying to say.

It was only on my long drive home that night that I began to feel uneasy with my response. First, it was not a thoughtful response or a response at all; it was a reaction, based on my assumptions about her and about my students' level of awareness in general. If I had stopped and *inquired* into what she meant, she would have told me that she had taught in rural northern Alaska where her Inuit students left school for weeks every fall to hunt for the moose that would sustain their families over the winter, and where the curriculum, aligned with tests devised for suburban White students in the lower 48, fell far short of meeting their needs. Why couldn't the curriculum and the structure of school reflect their lives, their particular circumstances, as IEPs are designed to meet students'? This was worth talking about and I regret having cut off a rich source of discussion, not to mention having put Helen on the defensive at best or, worse, silencing her. I emailed her the next day, apologizing, and asking to hear more of her story and point of view. The work of repair in the teacher–student relationship is vital to the functioning of a classroom (Rodgers & Raider-Roth, 2006).

Multiple I's

Each teacher enters the classroom with multiple I's in play. In other words, we carry within us multiple selves. I am a teacher, a researcher, a professional development provider, and a writer, but I am also a daughter, a sister, a wife, a mother, a mother-in-law, White, middle class, historically (and indelibly) WASP. Yet, this is not the whole of me. There are many "me's" that enter the room, some foregrounded, some happy to remain in the background, but all lurking.

Much has been written about the persons of the I and the Thou—multiple intelligence theory, Piagetian phases of intellectual development, attachment theory, theories of introversion and extroversion, Myers–Briggs personality inventories, and on and on. The literature on teacher identity is vast. In a review of this literature (Rodgers & Scott, 2008) we noted that contemporary conceptions of identity share four basic assumptions:

1. Identity is dependent upon and formed within multiple contexts that bring social, cultural, political, and historical forces to bear upon that formation.
2. Identity is formed in relationship with others and involves emotions.
3. Identity is shifting, unstable, and multiple.
4. Identity involves the construction and reconstruction of meaning through stories of self over time.

Implicit in the literature is that teachers should be aware of the complexity of any human being, including themselves. Developmentally speaking, cultivating awareness and bringing it to bear on one's actions is easier said than done. Nonetheless, the complexity is there, inviting our reflection.

At the beginning of many of the classes I teach, I have students introduce themselves from multiple angles—as teacher, student, learner, family member, athlete, reader, citizen, person of faith, race, and ethnicity. Finally, I have each student tell the story of their name. Some of these identities and stories are tender; therefore, I allow students to pass if they don't feel comfortable sharing. But the point I seek to make is that whenever they enter a classroom, they bring themselves with them. Likewise, so do their students. Everyone has a name and is made of many stories (see Adichie, 2009). It is why Cuban's designation of teaching as complex is so apt.

THE THOU (LEARNER)

The Use of "Thou"

There is no indication in Hawkins's work that he borrowed the term *Thou* from Martin Buber's (1923/1987) *I and Thou*. Hawkins also may have borrowed the term *Thou* from the Quaker tradition. It was introduced into the Quaker tradition in 17th-century England as a way of addressing individuals, no matter what their rank. At the time, only individuals of rank (e.g., lords, dames, judges) were addressed as "you." In an effort to recognize the spiritual equality of all persons, however, the Quakers insisted on addressing all individuals by Thou or Thee. This rankled the elite and got Quakers in a heap of trouble.

Buber's theology is a bit more complex. The pronoun "Thou" stands in contrast to the pronoun "it." Thou, Buber argued, is always in relation, in contrast to it, which is nothing more than "a thing." As humans, we always have the option of being in relationship, experiencing the spiritual in the other, whether the other is an element of the natural world or of the human world. We can choose to relate to either as an it or as a Thou, that is, an entity who is affected by us and who affects our own lives. I will say more about how an "it" can become a Thou below.

Thou as Learner

The primary role of the Thou is as learner, meaning-maker. Learners make meaning through interaction with the world. They do so with help from others but no one can learn for anyone but themselves. In her 1987 essay "Understanding Children's Understanding," Eleanor Duckworth addresses the importance of trusting students' power to make their own sense. She writes that teachers must make room to "give children reason," that is, to explore and understand their ways of making sense (p. 87). She tells the story of two boys, one of whom had been charged with the task of instructing the other in constructing a pattern from pattern blocks (colored triangles, squares, rectangles, trapezoids, and rhombuses). There was a screen between them, so that one had to listen carefully to the other as he followed his partner's directions. Teachers who later watched the videotape of the exchange saw that the boy doing the construction had great difficulty following the other boy's directions. They judged him dull, confused, slow. Upon reviewing the tape, however, their attention was directed to one piece of language. The boy giving the instructions had referred to a green square. In fact, there was no green square, only green triangles. The other boy, hearing green, grabbed the triangle and tried to make that instruction and all subsequent instructions work, but understandably with confusion and difficulty. Where the teachers before had judged the boy as slow, they now saw that he "had reason." They just needed to watch closely enough to see the construction of his understanding and the reasons behind it. Certainly, students make mistakes, but often they also are making their own kind of sense, if not ours.

Thou as Teacher

The learner, as I've said, is also a teacher. He has taught himself many things. He also has taught others, including the teacher, about himself, others, the world, as well as the subject matter at hand, about which he often comes knowing a lot and can perceive in ways that the teacher may never have thought of. The teacher can rely on students as knowers, as beings with imaginations, and as capable of helping others come to know. Students also come with their own "funds of knowledge" (Moll, Amanti, Neff, & González, 1992), rich sources of cultural and historical knowledge and skills that infuse their lives, and that are essential for individual and community functioning and well-being. If teachers listen, they can learn much from these sources.

Multiple Thous

Like the I, the Thou comes with its many identities and discourses, any one of which—or many of which—may show up on any given day. Like the teacher, the Thous too are shaped by many forces, from family to friends, worship place to playground, race, class, and gender stereotypes, class rank, reading level, skin tone, athletic ability, and on and on.

While there is usually just one teacher in a classroom, there is a multitude of Thous. As Figure 6.3 shows, each of these Thous is potentially in relationship with every other Thou. If there are three Thous, there are three potential paths of interaction; if there are four Thous, six pathways; five Thous, 10. If there are 20 students in the classroom, there are 209 possible pathways of interaction among them! It is why adding just one more student to the classroom is more than just +1. And, on any day, the Thou who

Figure 6.3. The Thou

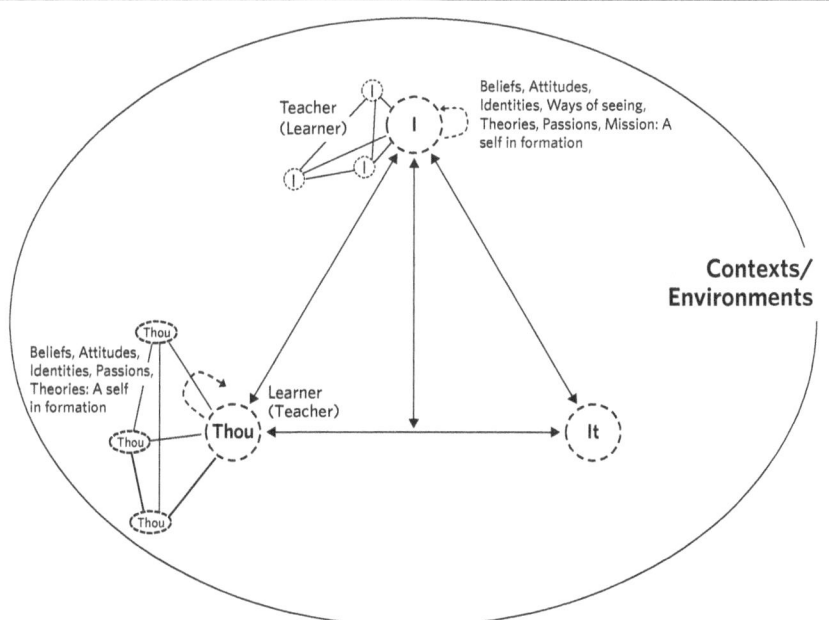

enters the classroom in the morning may, through the course of the events of the day, bear little resemblance to the Thou who leaves at its end. Not to mention a student's interactions with things: pencils, books, worksheets, erasers, and other small things that can be fiddled with and thrown. It is a small miracle that classroom management happens at all.

THE IT (CONTENT)

The third circle, the It, as shown in Figure 6.4, represents content, or subject matter. Hawkins (1974/2002) referred to the It as "the stuff of the world"— also the *"great It"* (emphasis in original), from which all subject matter comes. The world is not neatly divided into science, literature, math, or history. As I mentioned in the beginning chapters of this book, these are human constructs we've developed to organize, order, and manage our world. Each discipline helps us to explore the meaning of life from its own particular angle. Biology, for example, asks about organic life: What organisms exist? What are they made of? What do they do? How do they work? How do they interact? How do they live? How do they die? Literature interrogates the human experience through story: What makes us human? How are we human together? What shapes us? What makes us do what we do? Physics asks, What is energy? Where does it come from? How does it work? Is there

Figure 6.4. The It

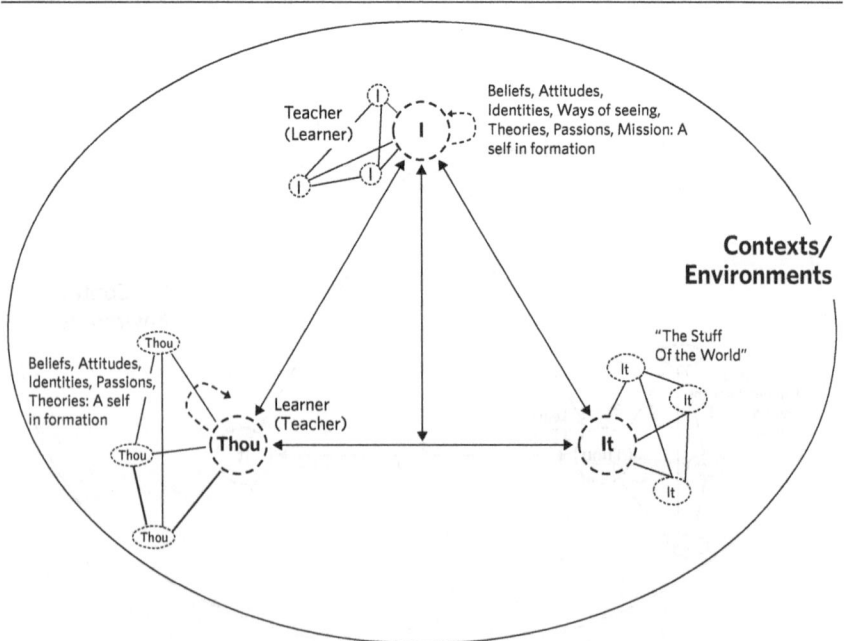

an edge to the universe? And so forth, in all the disciplines. (Never mind for the moment that these big questions tend to get lost in the disconnected facts that we ask students to remember.)

It is the world (and beyond our world)—what is and what might be—that is the real subject matter. As such, the various "Its" that are out there—the subjects kids study in schools—overlap and interweave in multiple ways (see the connecting lines between the Its). You cannot answer questions about global warming, for example, without also venturing into geography, economics, sociology, psychology, math, biology, and physics. In some ways, although understandable, the division of the world into separate subject areas is completely artificial and a bit crazy.

You will note that the circle of the It, like the large circles of I and Thou, as well as each of the smaller circles, is perforated. This is meant to suggest that as human beings we take the world into ourselves and are changed by that interaction, and, as we act upon the world, it too is changed. None of us is permanent or entirely stable or predictable. We are permeable.

While each element of the I, Thou, and It triangle is essential, the It was Hawkins's central concern. Without the It, the I and Thou have no reason to meet, he argued. Without an It, it is just an affair of mirrors—an I and Thou facing each other without a third ("It") to engage with. If the It is not engaging enough, the relationship between the I and the Thou tends to unravel, as any teacher can tell you. What makes the It engaging enough to sustain the integrity of this triangular relationship? According to Hawkins, there are several criteria, all of which are interconnected.

The Great It

First, subject matter is encountered in and derived from the world, embodied in phenomena. Generally, it is not to be found in a textbook, neatly organized. (Although it is found in literature and poetry, it still has meaning because of the experience of it.) It is textbooks, but in its abstracted form. The It surrounds us. We are in It. We *are* It. The It includes not just the concrete stuff of science and math (Hawkins's domain) but also ideas: democracy, justice, loss, love, leadership, and friendship. These phenomena may be ordered and explained in books, but they are not the thing itself any more than reading a driver's manual is the same thing as driving a car. The thing itself is embodied in phenomena—a leaf, the yearly journey of the earth around the sun, a metal boat that floats and a piece of metal that sinks, experiences of injustice and beauty.

Second, the learner who lives and learns in this phenomenal world, encounters the It, perforce, in all its complexity. Rather than reading a logical, ordered explanation of the revolution of the moon around the earth and the earth around the sun in an earth science textbook, where it is "detached from the process and order in which it has been evolved," learners have the capacity to uncover this planetary story, reconstructing (with guidance from a good teacher) these movements in their own mind and with their own hands and bodies (Hawkins, 1974/2002, p. 98).

Third, while these phenomena represent mysterious stories to be unraveled, they are also comfortingly familiar. They include things like a tree, a mirror, stones to be counted, unfairness, loss, discrimination. A learner looks into the sky and recognizes the shimmery crescent she has seen since she can remember and that has appeared in her books and drawings. She looks at herself in the mirror every morning. She counts marbles and candy and fingers and days. She plays with things that float and sink in the bathtub. She is bullied on the playground, loses a pet or a grandparent, witnesses the seasons. Yet as she looks more closely, these familiar things can become strange, curious, interesting, and full of mystery that has not been visible before. Where does that shadow on the moon come from? Why do we have day and night? Why can she see in the bathroom mirror that tree that is completely out of her line of sight? Why do bullies bully? Why do people get old or sick and die?

Organization of the It

The organization inherent in subject matter is not at first apparent to the learner. The process of discovering such order constitutes what Hawkins terms the "aesthetic." It includes that internal motivation to explore, "a mode of behavior in which the distinction between ends and means collapses; it is its own end and it is its own reinforcement" (2000, p. 116). An order emerges, but it is not the predetermined order of a distant textbook writer or curriculum specialist. It is an aesthetic that belongs both to the subject matter and to the learner. Witness Oliver Sacks's (1999) "discovery" of the Periodic Table:

> It was only when I had the concept of atomic weight firmly in mind, along with the concept of atoms' combining power, or valency, that I could appreciate the startling beauty, the obvious truth, of the Periodic Table—for me, now, the most beautiful thing in the world. (p. 70)

This understanding arrived far down the road from Sacks's original experiences with minerals, metals, and chemicals. It grew *out of* those experiences. Dewey (1902) called this trek from undifferentiated experience to organized abstract knowledge the continuum from the psychological to the logical. The psychological is embodied in experience—the world encountered whole, in all its complexity. The logical is the experience reorganized and reconstructed into categories and themes that give it order and serve as a framework for further understanding. We might say, then, that subject matter that is engaging must be embodied in phenomena, complex and familiar, and that most subject matter has an inherent order, patterns, and themes that, although painful at times to extract, also can be experienced as "beautiful."

Because the It encompasses everything, it also encompasses both the I and the Thou, as well as all the contextual elements and forces that surround them. In a sense, the whole picture collapses upon itself into one "great It." This merits attention. It reminds both students and teachers that school is about Life, the Big Questions that matter to children and should matter to adults. Being educated is not about being master of all the little "facts, facts, *facts*!" as Dickens's (1854/2007) teacher from *Hard Times*, Mister M'Choakumchild, would have it:

> So, Mr. M'Choakumchild began in his best manner. He and some one hundred and forty other schoolmasters, had been lately turned at the same time, in the same factory, on the same principles, like so many pianoforte legs. He had been put through an immense variety of paces, and had answered volumes of head-breaking questions. Orthography, etymology, syntax, and prosody, biography, astronomy, geography, and general cosmography, the sciences of compound proportion, algebra, land-surveying and leveling, vocal music, and drawing from models, were all at the ends of his ten chilled fingers. He had worked his stony way into Her Majesty's most Honourable Privy Council's Schedule B, and had taken the bloom off the higher branches of mathematics and physical science, French, German, Latin, and Greek. He knew all about all the Water Sheds of all the world (whatever they are), and all the histories of all the peoples, and all the names of all the rivers and mountains, and all the productions, manners, and customs of all the countries, and all their boundaries and bearings on the two and thirty points of the compass. (pp. 48–49)

By the end of that paragraph you can feel the weight of those facts! But being educated is not the accumulation of facts; it is continuous discovery of all the *connections* among life's infinite phenomena, seeing and experiencing them in new ways, feeling both humbled in the face of their inexhaustibility, and at home as a part of it all. We are, as Hawkins said, all in *It* together.

CHAPTER 7

The Teaching Triangle

Its Dynamics

THE I-THOU DYNAMIC

The expertise of teachers resides in their skill in navigating the dynamics of the I, Thou, and It. The I–Thou bidirectional axis (see Figure 7.1) represents a relationship between human beings, with all the complexities that that suggests. When both selves—the teacher's and the student's—are fully present, particularly around a third, engaging It, the classroom comes alive. It is, in fact, the It that is key. Finding the things that ignite those essential aspects of self—curiosity, wonder, bafflement, recognition, sympathy, humor—leads to wanting to know more. The teacher must have studied her students, "learned" them, to know what things might open these doors to the students' selves. It is why the first day of class is both so exciting and so scary for a teacher and her students. Who are these selves? How do I connect to them? And, if I don't do so quickly, things may fall apart.

It is a sort of catch-22. In order to form the strong I–Thou connection necessary for a well-functioning classroom, I need to offer various Its that engage students and bring them alive. In order to know which Its will do this, I, the teacher, need to know my Thous. This is why I spend the first several hours of class time building community and suggest to teachers that a day or a week spent building community is a month of saved time in trying to build and rebuild trust. There is a multitude of games and activities (often in the form of icebreakers) out there, online and in books. I find theater games to be particularly effective in cutting through inhibitions and shyness, and opening up individuals to being known and being themselves. Merely rolling out these activities probably won't work, but connecting them clearly to the goal of building community, and a clear vision of and commitment to why community matters in learning, will. Learners know this intuitively. Being explicit about it lends logical shape to that psychological experience.

For me, community, the strengthening of all relational ties, matters for several reasons. On the individual level, each student, in order to learn, must feel safe—to speak out, to take risks, to interact with peers without being put down, to be listened to and seen. At the interpersonal level, because learning happens not solely from reading but from discussion and

Figure 7.1. The I–Thou

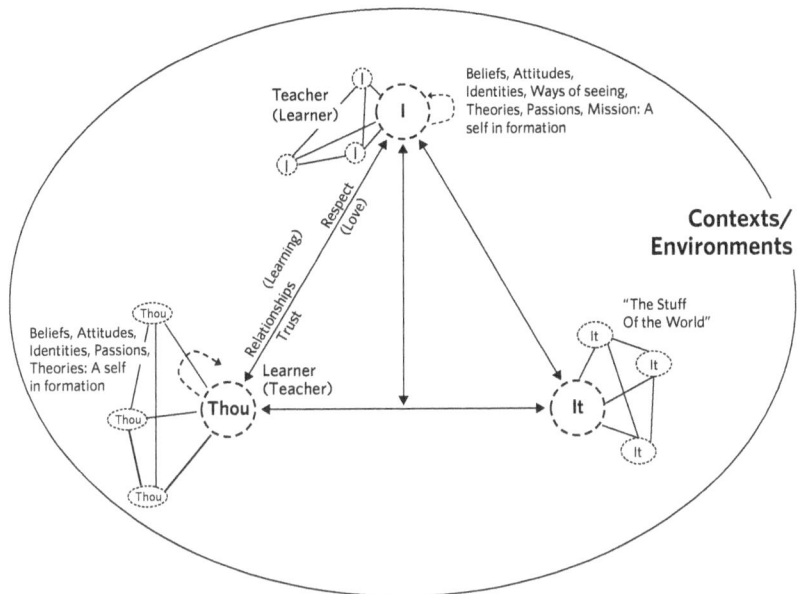

investigation *with* others, trust in one another is essential. Finally, learning as a community in the classroom also should prepare students to be community members outside the classroom, to be participants in a democracy. This is as true for online learning as it is for face-to-face learning. Dewey's (1916) words warrant a close and careful read:

> Democracy is more than a form of government; it is primarily a mode of associated living, of conjoint communicated experience. The extension in space of the number of individuals who participate in an interest so that each has to refer his own action to that of others, and to consider the action of others to give point and direction to his own, is equivalent to the breaking down of those barriers of class, race, and national territory which kept [people] from perceiving the full import of their activity. (p. 93)

It is this larger goal of a vibrant democracy that both grounds what otherwise might seem like silly icebreakers and provides what Dewey calls an "end-in-view" to which to aspire. As a class's time together rolls out, the activities that are offered by the teacher will either continue to bind them or leave them as loosely associated beings. As Dewey (1916) writes, "In order to have a large number of values in common, all the members of the group must have an equable opportunity to receive and to take from others. There must be a large variety of shared undertakings and experiences" (p. 90).

It is, in fact, the shared undertakings and experiences that bind them. In other words, the I–Thou and Thou–Thou relationships grow out of shared encounters with the It.

At the heart of this relationship, as Hawkins has said, is (ideally) respect. To have respect for what the learner brings, implies that a teacher begins there and does not assume that the learner is a proverbially empty vessel or blank slate, knowing nothing of the subject matter at hand. The teacher respects the capacities that a learner brings. I once asked my son, then beginning 9th grade, what his ideal teacher would do. "Three things," he told me without hesitation. The first one was, *"Find out what I already know."* (He said it with italics in his voice.) The other two were, "Take me outside," and "Give me choices." Respect for what a learner *already* knows is essential to the I–Thou relationship. No one likes to be instructed in what they already know— asked, yes; told, no. More important, finding the edge of students' learning gives a teacher the starting point(s) for her teaching. Keeping students always on that edge keeps them alert and alive. Too far back from the edge and they are bored. Too far over the edge and they fall. Both cause them to retreat.

Being offered a challenge that extends the knowledge and capacities of the learner engenders, in turn, a learner's respect for the teacher. This mutual respect is a dynamic, (co)constructive force wherein teacher and students build new understandings that eventually lead to the teacher making herself obsolete. As Hawkins says: "The teacher offers the learner a kind of loan of her self, some kind of auxiliary equipment that will enable the learner to make transitions and consolidations not otherwise possible. And if this equipment is of a kind to be itself internalized, the learner not only learns but begins, in the process, to become a self-teacher—and that is how the loan is repaid" (p. 44).

Hawkins (1974/2002) theorized that a teacher's effectiveness and authority are embedded in the relationships that she builds with her students. They build a compact of trust resulting from the learners' experience of having learned, of feeling the extension and deepening of their selves and their own power to make sense of and control their world.

The trust between teacher and students is earned each day but can be easily lost if not tended to. The good news is that a breach in trust can be repaired. My colleague, Miriam Raider-Roth, writes that the teacher–learner relationship, like the parent–child relationship, benefits from a process of "mutual regulation." Parents and children learn to read one another and adjust their actions in accordance with the responses they perceive. Similarly, as the teacher and student learn what it takes to reconnect, they build the foundation of trust in their relationship (Rodgers & Raider-Roth, 2006). It is not avoiding ruptures in trust that matters, for these are inevitable; it is building the capacity for repair.

The example cited above, where I described my cutting a student off and then emailing her the following day, is a case in point. As noted, I emailed Helen the following morning, saying, in part:

Reflecting on my response, I wish that I had inquired more into your idea and not reacted so quickly with a cautionary tone, stemming from my own assumptions about your assumptions about low-income schools. I think that I may have put you in an awkward position, where you then had to defend your idea. I regret having put you in that position instead of finding out more about what you were thinking. It's one of those ground rules that we generated that I then violated. So, my apologies for that. I would also love to hear more about your time in Alaska and L.A. schools, which I am sure raised a lot of fascinating questions for you and your husband about schools.

In thinking this incident through further, and in discussion with a teacher of mindfulness practice, I was able to see further into my own reactions following the class. Two mindfulness concepts, moral shame and moral dread, were very helpful in making sense of my experience. Moral shame (*hiri*) refers to an immediate sense of remorse, a physical recognition that one has done harm. The shame I felt was a signal from my own moral compass that I had wandered off course and needed to take action to realign. The second feeling, moral dread (*ottappa*), refers to my sense of shame at having violated a public trust and my own integrity. As a class we had developed norms, which included this one: "Seek to understand a thought before judging and responding to what you *think* someone has said. Inquire into it to understand it better and make sure your assumptions about what has been said are correct." I had violated that shared, co-constructed norm and in doing so risked losing the trust of the class as well as my own integrity as a teacher.

THE I–IT DYNAMIC

No teacher is worth her salt who is not able to confront students with a rigorous body of knowledge. (Paolo Freire as told to Joe Kincheloe, 2008, p. 21)

Unless the teacher's mind has mastered the subject matter in advance, unless it is thoroughly at home in it, using it unconsciously without the need of express thought, he will not be free to give full time and attention to observation and interpretation of the pupils' intellectual reactions. (Dewey, 1933, p. 275)

Both Freire and Dewey clearly imply that for the I to be present to the Thou, the I must be thoroughly prepared, not just with subject matter knowledge, but with the curriculum, appropriate methods, and relevant activities. The teacher, ideally, is constantly developing her relationship with the subject matter she teaches, deepening it, and broadening her perception of the connections between it and other knowledge (see Figure 7.2). But in the classroom her attention is with what the learner is doing with the subject matter.

In order to create a curriculum and construct activities that engage students, she is required not only to understand her subject matter but also to understand that subject matter from a naïve perspective. She must be alert to how her learners make sense of the world, to all the ways that they might see it. To be able to anticipate these ways of seeing, and learn about them through observing and asking, is an essential part of the I–It relationship. As Hawkins writes, teachers must anticipate "the process and order in which [subject matter] has been evolved and, more importantly, form the diverse sorts of process and order by which it might be evolved again in the minds of individual learners" (2000, pp. 98–99). Imagining these "diverse sorts of process and order," inherent in subject matter, a teacher can more easily conceive of its various potential entry points.

The art of pedagogy comes in being able to translate these points of entry into activities and link these activities to the minds and abilities of children. No teacher's guide or curricular textbook can possibly determine ahead of time this trajectory for any one child, much less a group of them. Texts can serve as resources, but not step-by-step guides. It is the children and their learning that are the guides, that give the teacher the necessary clues about when and how and how much to intervene.

Figure 7.2. The I–It

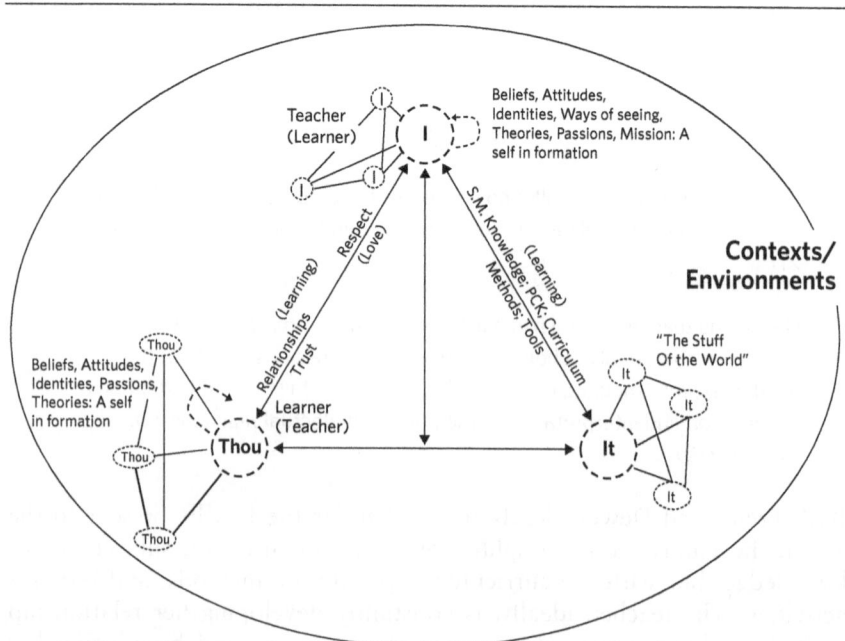

To carry out that agenda, the teacher draws upon various tools and resources, from the Internet to Cuisenaire rods, from simulations to fieldtrips. Ideally, the way a teacher teaches, the organization of the curriculum, the methods, techniques, activities, and tools she uses align with one another and with her own beliefs about teaching and learning and the purpose of school.

THE THOU-IT DYNAMIC

Now we move to the relationship that defines the purpose of schooling—that between the learner and the world he is learning about, the Thou–It, the bottom line of the triangle (see Figure 7.3). This relationship speaks to the basis of the contract between teacher and student: that students will learn.

There are plenty of classrooms where this relationship is indirect, where the subject matter is transmitted through the teacher, rather than being experienced directly by the learner. For me, the greatest challenge of teaching is how to put learners in *direct rather than indirect* contact with their world (i.e., to provide them with *experiences*), then to support them in making sense of the world they encounter and of which they are a part. My goal is that they feel that the world has something to do with them, and they with the world. This means they must grapple with the as-yet unknown. Researcher Alan Schoenfeld (2014) has called such grappling "productive struggle."

Figure 7.3. The Thou–It

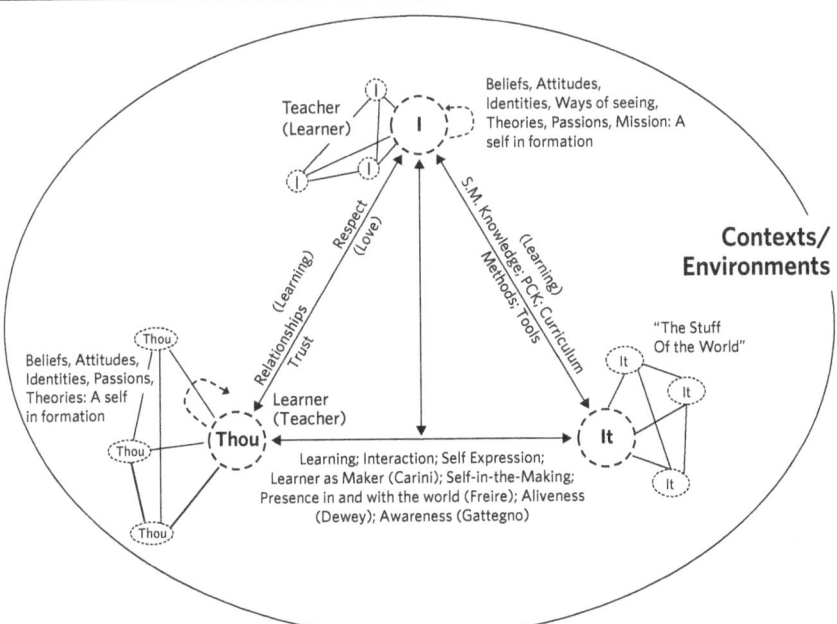

Even subject matter that seems remote and abstract can be imagined into a more immediate experience for students, granting them an on-ramp to more rarified concepts. Experience can be in the moment and real, but it also can be recollected, represented, pictured, and acted out. For example, asking students to think of a time when they experienced being silenced by someone more powerful than themselves, as a portal to larger ideas like oppression and colonialism, changes something that can feel remote into something real and personal. This is not to equate small episodes of silencing with the history of colonialism, but to take that seed of under-standing and grow it into a sturdy tree of understanding, compassion, commitment, and agency. Freire's (1970/2011) method of "problem pos-ing" utilizes such a model. Using drawings and other kinds of "codes" to represent experience, he extends the personal and particular into the uni-versal and general. The body also can be used to stand in for realities that cannot be directly experienced. For example, in our study of the moon, I have students use their bodies to act out the movements of the Earth, sun, and moon.[3]

In the school in the Bronx where I work, children use Cuisenaire rods to learn how math and number actually work, and Words in Color charts to learn the complexities of sound–letter relationships. Both of these sets of tools allow students to directly experience phenomena (number and the written word) of our cultural worlds.[4] In the same school, one 4th-grade social studies teacher introduced students to the idea of taxation without representation by giving them "cash" in the form of pretend paper money. They then had to pay for certain privileges like using the pencil sharpener, going to the bathroom, turning on the lights, even raising their hands. They felt the unfairness of it and were then prepared to investigate what the colo-nists in 18th-century Boston did in response to their experience of taxation. The ways of experiencing subject matter are as unlimited as the teacher's imagination.

In the Thou–It exchange, the logic of the It is slowly uncovered by the Thou. There develops a relationship between them that can be powerful, even passionate, and affectionate. I take as an example my teaching of the moon. We spend about an hour a week in class for nearly a full semester studying it. Outside of class, students first must hunt it down in the sky. Where do they need to look for it? It was there last night at this time; why is it missing tonight? Where does it go? They discover that it also appears in the daytime. After weeks of observing the moon—drawing what they see; recording data like time and the moon's angle above the horizon; sharing their observations; being moon, sun, and Earth with their bodies; figuring out its orbit around the Earth, why it disappears for about 4 days in its approximately 28-day cycle; why there are phases, and so much more—they have formed a relationship with the moon. Some come to refer to it as "she." "I saw her last night! She was just a sliver hanging in the western sky." By the end of the semester students have, effectively, transformed the

"It" of the moon into a "Thou." Careful attention to and interaction with the It will do that.

This transformation of the external world from informational to soulful, from *apart from* oneself to *a part of* oneself, is, I believe, vital to the survival of the planet and our common humanity. This is true not only when the subject matter is lovely, like the moon. It is true also for subject matter that includes atrocities, like war and oppression. To see all of the world as a part of all of us is to be educated. As Martha Nussbaum (2010) has put it, "When we meet in society, if we have not learned to see both self and other [as human], imagining in one another inner faculties of thought and emotion, democracy is bound to fail, because democracy is built upon respect and concern, and these in turn are built upon the ability to see other people as human beings, not simply as objects" (p. 6). Multiple-choice tests will never get us there. As one 5th-grade child at the Bronx Charter School so wisely put it, "Kids will never understand fully if you just tell them the answer, they have to break it down and understand it, take it piece by piece, 'cuz if you get it straight on, you'll never know what happened. Like, if you're building something you'll never understand how it's built, you'll never build it again, because you don't know what to do." Again, it falls upon the teacher to create experiences that will give kids the opportunity to break it down and understand it, to "take it piece by piece."

THE I'S INTERACTION WITH THE THOU–IT DYNAMIC

The vertical arrow down the middle of the triangle shown in Figure 7.4, which connects the teacher (I) with the Thou–It dynamic, speaks to what the teacher does from moment to moment in teaching—what Donald Schön (1983) calls *reflection-in-action*. If the teacher has set an activity for students to *do*, then there is something there to observe, and observation becomes a primary task. Again, if delivery of material by the teacher (teacher-centered "telling" or what Freire calls the "banking" method of teaching) is primary, the teacher is doing most of the "doing" and not only is there less to observe but her energy is focused on the subject matter (It) rather than the learning (Thou–It).

But observation alone is not enough. What a teacher sees as she observes must be interpreted or, as Hawkins puts it, "diagnosed." (The term *diagnosis* has been criticized by some as a medical term pointing to problems or sickness. I see it much more broadly, in terms of analysis and interpretation.)

Hawkins (1974/2002) writes:

What seems very clear to me . . . is that if you operate a school [or classroom] . . . in such a style that the children are rather passively sitting in neat rows and columns and manipulating you into believing that they're being attentive

Figure 7.4. The I's Interaction with the Thou–It Dynamic

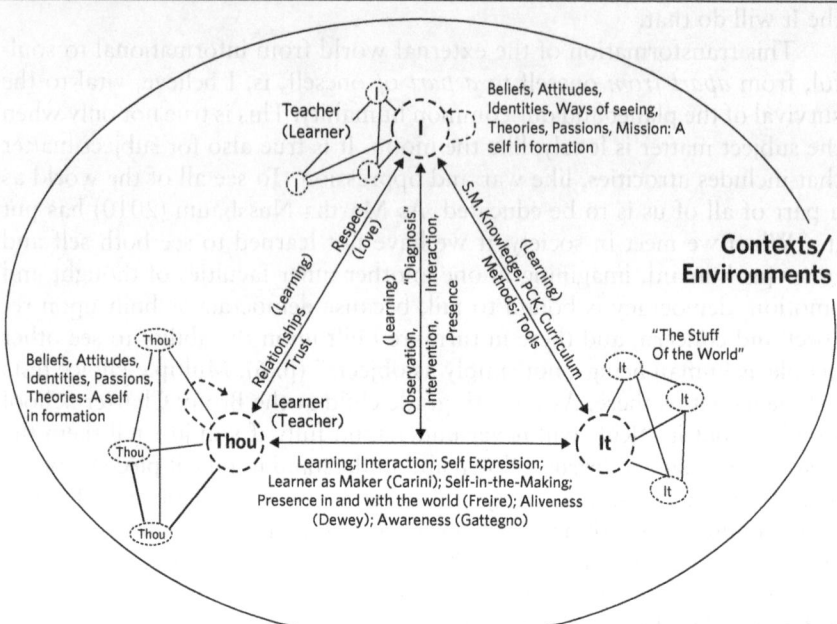

because they're not making any trouble, then you won't get very much information about them. Not getting much information about them, you won't be a very good diagnostician. Not being a good diagnostician, you will be a poor teacher. The child's overt involvement in a rather self-directed way, using the big muscles and not just the small ones, is most important to the teacher in providing an input of information wide in range and variety. It is input which potentially has much more heft than what you can possibly get from the merely verbal or written responses of a child to questions put to him or tasks set for him. When we fail in this diagnostic role we begin to worry about "assessment." (p. 57)

I maintain that this is as true for adults learning at the college level as it is for children. It is through exploration and inquiry, constructing, taking apart, and reconstructing, making and correcting mistakes, that the person and the subject matter are revealed, not just to the teacher, but to the learner himself. There is a sense of aliveness, discovery of the world and oneself simultaneously, self-expression where that expression is a discovery and a documentation of a self-in-the-making, a new awareness and expansion of both the world and oneself. What a privilege to witness! And what a responsibility to make happen. For me, harkening back to the I–It, this is where the teacher's imagination comes into play. I need to imagine how each of my students sees the world and then imagine the portals I might provide that will invite them to venture in and spark their own questions. This provides ongoing feedback about what students know, understand, and can do, so that we are not left to wait until the test to know what they know.

That said, it is also true that the subject matter can come alive through the teacher's passion, love, and enthusiasm for it. The teacher herself can be the way in. At the same time, at some point, the learners must craft their own relationship to the content, even if it is forever infused with the energy of the teacher. The learner becomes the knower and can, in turn, pay that passion forward to others.

Based on what a teacher sees and hears and senses (observation), and the sense that she makes of that (diagnosis/interpretation), she chooses when and how to intervene (or not). Intervention can come in the form of questions, instructions, additional information, or a decision to re-teach or to stop a lesson. It can happen at the large-group, small-group, or individual level. Every intervention is, in a sense, an experiment; the teacher watches to see what happens next and decides whether to intervene again.

I would characterize the whole of this line (the I to the Thou–It) as "presence." It is, in fact, the whole of reflection in a moment.

SUMMARY OF THE I, THOU, AND IT

The I, Thou, and It map, with its nodes and axes, provides a way of naming, seeing, and breaking down the complexities of practice. It allows one to ask, What happened in class? What did I see? Where was my attention? What did I *not* see, *not* pay attention to? What was going on inside of me, emotionally and cognitively? What did I do? What sense were students making of the content? What did they do? What was going on inside of them? What did they learn? How do I know? What's my evidence?

While it all looks very symmetrical and neatly laid out (more or less) in the diagrams, the trouble is, it all takes place within multiple, very powerful contextual forces that shape what happens inside and between nodes. I move next to an exploration of these forces.

CHAPTER 8

Context

> When teachers do not contextualize they tend to isolate various parts of a
> pedagogical circumstance and call each a problem. (Bohm & Edwards, 1991,
> as cited in Kincheloe, 2008, p. 33)

CONTEXT AS A SYSTEM

The forces of context in Figure 8.1 are represented by wavy lines and arrows surrounding the triangle. While they are individually labeled, they are
a connected system rather than discreet forces. They often are referred to as
the "hidden curriculum." You will see that they include everything from educational policy decisions like state testing, standards, and tenure policies,
to the forces of home and family, the physical spaces where learning happens (desks, classrooms, resources), the politics of a community, state, and
nation—even global politics—and the deeply embedded forces of history,
economics, and race, class, and gender, among other socio-cultural forces.
These forces can, and do, distort the triangle and the potential relationships
along each axis, as well as the size and strength of each node.

Hawkins does not deal with these powerful realities in his essay, but
they are as much a part of the picture, literally in this case, as everything
else. Sometimes, because these forces can be so strong, even overwhelming,
they become the *only* part of the picture, or certainly the dominant part.

What I am attempting to do is to name these things so they can become
objects of reflection. When we can perceive these forces as objects we can
name and hold, rather than faceless forces that control us, it allows us some
degree of control. Naming the world, as Freire (1970/2011) says, is the first
step in getting a handle on it and gaining some agency over it: "To exist
humanly, is to *name* the world, to change it" (p. 88, emphasis in original).
Or, as Robert Kegan (1982) has put it, instead of unconsciously operating
under the power of our perceptions, being *subject* to them, our perceptions
can become *objects* of our attention.

A story of the forces of context at work comes from my early days of
teaching. I was a Peace Corps volunteer teaching English in a boys' lycée
in the city of Saint Louis, Sénégal, a longtime French colony. The school
was the oldest such school in West Africa (so old, in fact, that one day a

Figure 8.1. Contexts/Environments

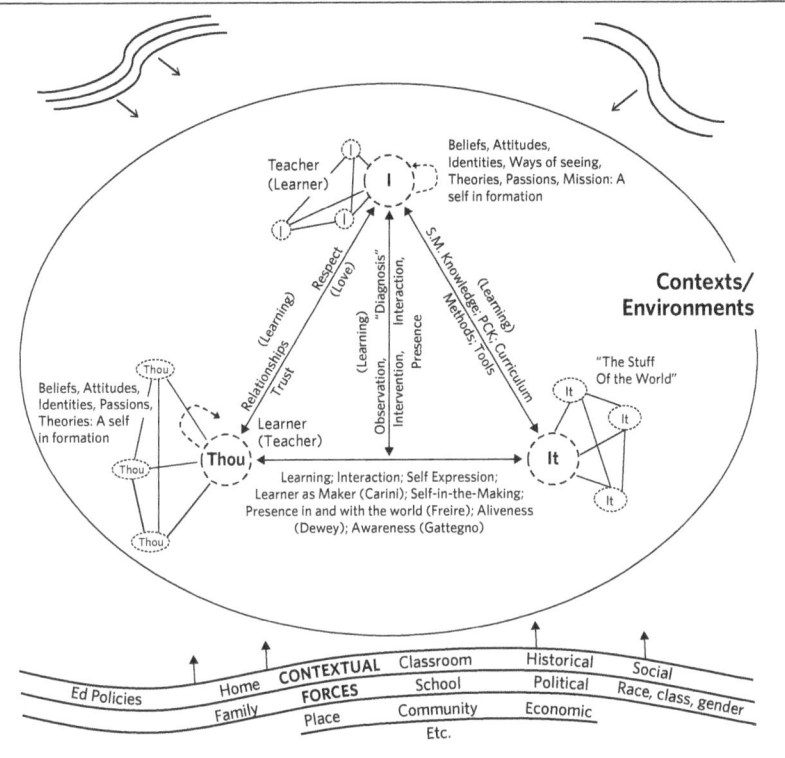

classroom ceiling collapsed when a fighter jet flew overhead). Midyear I inherited a class of 60 boys, ranging in age from 15 to 17, that had gone without a teacher for the first 3 weeks of the term. By the time I got them they were, well, accustomed to their freedom. I tried teaching them, but even if I had the attention of 30 of them, the 30 in the back were lost to me.

This class gave me stomachaches. I so dreaded going in to work that some days I would send word that I was sick. I certainly felt sick. No matter what I tried, no matter my one year of experience and relative success, I was not able to connect with this group. From my perspective, I was trying my darnedest, and they were not trying at all. I felt they saw me as a non-person, and I frankly was beginning to see them as a singular monster, not as individual human beings but as a single-minded menace.

Eventually, I decided to split the class into two sections and see each section every other day. I did this without asking permission to do so; the school was so arbitrary in its management that no one seemed to notice. Students came and went without any real supervision. My adjustments cut down on the chaos, but did little to heal the animosity that had grown between the students and me. Language was a barrier as neither my French nor my Wolof was good enough to make inroads, or command respect, and their English was equally lacking. What's more, their motivation for learning English was, understandably, nonexistent. I just could not seem to find common ground where we might have met.

Finally the end of the term arrived. I gave them their final exam, knowing that they had not learned what I would be testing them on, even though I had taught it, or tried to. Sure enough, nearly half the class failed. A hard, mean, little part of me was happy. I would finally have the upper hand. What happened next still haunts me—not so much because of what happened to me, but because of what I did to them.

Several days after the exam, all final grades (from all classes) were posted, publicly, on the outside walls of the school. Classes had finished, but students were still around. I came into school the morning that grades were posted, probably to clear out my things. I approached the front door through the small courtyard, which was surrounded by a wall upon which sat a handful of boys. Suddenly, these boys, about a dozen of them, jumped off the wall and surrounded me. I didn't know what they were saying but it was clearly hostile, and I understood enough to know that it was about their grades. Two of them held a large palm frond in front of me, which prevented me from moving forward. Then I started to feel rocks being thrown at my ankles and I began to get scared.

I am not sure how long this lasted, but I remember hearing the voice of someone I trusted, the grounds keeper, N'Diaye, whom I greeted each morning, using my limited but improving Wolof, and who had always been kind to me. He was only about 5'3", but he had the authority of an adult male, and he told the boys to stop, which they did, slowly. I was rattled.

I recall thinking several things, most of them defensive. First, of course, I was scared, but then, immediately, I was angry at having been deeply wronged. I immediately appealed to the principal, who had nothing to say, literally. He shrugged his shoulders to let me know that there was nothing to be done. My second thought, still about me, was that these students did not know me. I was a good teacher, I had friends, people at home who loved me, and I had only done what they had forced me to do. I checked to make sure my identity, like a good suit, had no tears and was intact.

These rationalizations were acts of self-preservation. Only years later was I able to make sense of the incident in a way that did not ascribe blame to the students, the school, or myself. Now I am able to see that what happened was the result of many contextual forces, forces that shaped my perception of the students and the situation, as well as the students' perceptions of me—what Buddhists helpfully call "causes and conditions." As Joseph Goldstein (2013) writes, "Perceptions are not absolutes, they are conditioned on different levels. One of the great misconceptions we often carry throughout our lives is that our perceptions of ourselves and the world are basically accurate and true, that they reflect some stable, ultimate reality"

(p. 216). At the time, my perceptions did not extend beyond my own notions of fairness and civility—I did my best, and that should be good enough for "them." I "deserved," out of fairness, as good as I gave. But there were other conditions in play that I was oblivious to.

One "condition" that I did not see at the time—1978—was the very recent and centuries-long colonial history, including slavery, from which Sénégal was still emerging. How did I miss that one? (Hint: White privilege.) A second cultural condition was the patriarchal context in which I taught. Not only was I White and Western, embodying the recent colonial past, I was a woman and therefore in a default, one-down position. In addition, I was young, just 24. Just as important were the conditions under which my students learned and lived. These included the very real poverty and challenging living situations that many of them struggled with on a daily basis. Not all of my students were local. Many of them were from villages far from the city and lived in Saint Louis with distant family members, often as workers within the family. I later learned that some studied in the light of streetlamps at night. They were far from their families and their homes, and, in addition, carried with them their villages' expectations that as "educated" they eventually would support their extended families. In addition, some of them were forced to speak in second and third languages, not in their mother tongue.

A final condition, of which I was totally ignorant at the time, was that, according to the French educational policies that schools followed, when students failed a course, they failed the entire grade, which they then had to repeat. Given the expectations some of these boys carried from home, this could mean not returning to school at all and returning home shamed. No wonder they were angry.

If I had been more aware of these contextual forces, I like to think that I would have better understood the regard (or lack thereof) in which I was held, and would have behaved differently, more compassionately, and with greater equanimity than I did. I think that one indicator of an "equanimous mind" is awareness that causes and conditions are always in play. It is our job to inquire into and understand them as best we can.

While my identity as a good teacher remained intact, my stance at the time was one of self-justification rather than compassion born of critical reflection. I never bothered to ask, "What are the causes and conditions, the contextual forces, at work here? How are students perceiving the situation? I seem to have survived. How are they?" My perceptions, as far as I was concerned, were the whole of reality, rather than, as Goldstein (2013) says, "relative and limited" (p. 216).

PURPOSES OF EDUCATION

One of the hidden contextual forces in play in the United States is the assumed purpose of education held by society. Why are we in school in the first place? These purposes are rarely discussed critically outside of circles of research, but they shape the dynamics of the classroom as much as anything else. An example of the deeply embedded nature of these assumptions can be found in the interviews done by my graduate students of their students, children, families, neighbors, and friends. The students' task is to determine what various people, all of whom have attended years of school, see as the purpose of school. Almost without exception respondents give variations of the following answer: "To get into college, and to get a good job," or, in education-speak, "college and career." I once asked the principal at my own children's elementary school what he saw as the purpose of school. The question flummoxed him, as though I'd asked him what the purpose of breathing was. He answered with a tautology: "To have your kids do well in school." The purpose of school in most people's minds, is, vaguely, to move up to the next level of school successfully, graduate, and have a good life. Thoughts about why a society might need an educated populace usually don't come up.

An example of how this view plays itself out in school comes from a college freshman I once taught, whom I will call Amanda. One day Amanda came to my office in tears because she felt I was standing between her and her American Dream (her words). Amanda was a student in my seminar on John Dewey, which was offered to students in the Honors College. She was getting a B, an apparently new and upsetting experience for her. The reading, writing, and analysis I was asking students to do required them to use evidence drawn both from Dewey's texts and from their own experience. There was no answer key. It was a different kind of thinking for many of these honors students, accustomed as they were to five-paragraph essays and a skillful reiteration of what the teacher had taught.

Another student in the class, Natasha, was aware of this. An astute young immigrant from the West Indies, she came to see her secondary and elementary school experiences and those of her classmates, all Honors College students, this way: "In school we were very obedient children." In one paper, she recalled her own experiences as an elementary student in Queens, NY:

> As a lesson is being taught in class, I always have something in
> my mind that I am questioning or relating to from my personal
> experience. Sometimes I add my own ideas to this lesson but only in
> my mind, not aloud. My question differs from the teacher's question
> and my thoughts differ from the teacher's thought. We are innately
> different. My teacher sees the material one way, I see it another. So, I
> assume my way of seeing it is wrong.

As a child, Natasha learned to quash her own "wrong" thoughts and subsume them under the teacher's "right" thoughts—to be "obedient." She felt deeply the disconnection between her own ways of thinking and speaking (in a West Indies patois) and those of her teachers, one of whom told her she did not speak "proper English." But through reading Dewey's work, our discussions in class, and reflection on her past experiences, Natasha was able to reframe her experience as one of "obedience." She was able to take a critical stance toward her experience, see the oppression built into the status quo, question it, recast it, and identify a different purpose for her own schooling going forward. She could speak in *her* voice and learn who she *was* rather than wasn't.

By contrast, Amanda clung to the "obedient child" identity. She had accepted (probably unconsciously) that the purpose of school was not to think and speak her own thoughts, but to learn the teachers' thoughts. She had made it into the Honors College on the strength of those skills. Following all the rules, she banked on continuing down that path directly to her future. Yet, here I was, negating the playbook, standing in the way, claiming those rules did not apply. "All I want to do," she sobbed, "is get a 4.0, graduate from college, get a good job, have a family, and buy a house! I hate this course!" No doubt. Although this was a potentially rich teaching moment, she was not yet in a space where she was willing or able to question her decisions and beliefs, ones that had served her well. (And who was I to deny her that?) At least in the 3 months that I had her in my class, her views did not change. But that's so often the thing about teaching: You never really know how or whether you have mattered.

I cannot blame Amanda for clinging to these goals. They represent the purposes that society currently holds for schools. Indeed "obedience" is valued by most institutions. While we may espouse the desire to educate independent thinkers and citizens who can contribute to a diverse democracy, the underlying purposes of college and career—the hidden curriculum—come through loud and clear.

Purposes are, essentially, our theories of why we do what we do, including beliefs about teaching and learning and school. Chris Argyris and Donald Schön (1974) have identified two levels of theory/beliefs that are especially useful when it comes to thinking about teaching: "espoused theories" and "theories-in-use." Espoused theories are generally unassailable and what we like to broadcast to the world. Theories-in-use, in contrast, represent the truth about ourselves as practitioners and as a society.

An example of an espoused theory comes out of reactions to the racially motivated, anti-Semitic protests and their counterprotests in Charlottesville, Virginia (August 11 and 12, 2017). Subsequent to the violence, one group, which operated under the hash tag "#ThisIsNotUs," tweeted messages of resistance to the violence. Their assertion, "This is not us," although laudable, is really an *aspiration*—an espoused theory about who we *want* to be. Too often, such espoused theories are seen as sufficient but actually can represent an abdication of responsibility, as though pure intentions were enough. Jelani Cobb, an African American writer for *The New Yorker*, felt this contradiction and wrote this tweet in response: "People are saying this is not us. Of course it is. Refusing to grapple with that fact is how we got here in the first place." His statement represents a clear-headed awareness of a theory-in-use: that the actions of the White Nationalists/Nazis/Ku Klux Klan in Charlottesville *are* who we are as a society at a profound level, with our racist history, legacy of slavery, and systemic embrace of White Christian privilege and entitlement, even as the majority decries these actions. Until we acknowledge these theories-in-use, Cobb argues, we cannot move toward change.

Similarly, while we might espouse a particular set of beliefs about the purpose of school, that is, to educate citizens to participate in a democracy, what we ask teachers and students to *do* in school—how we ask them to spend their time—says much more about our theories-in-use, our "real theories": that the purpose of teaching is to get students to do well enough on tests that they can move on to the next grade, get into a good middle school/high school/college, get a good job, and earn enough money to live and provide for their families. There is nothing inherently wrong with these purposes, but they seem limited to many of us, with a purely functional view of what it means to educate a human being. It is my hope that the I, Thou, and It/Context framework can provide a tool for checking for alignment between one's espoused theories/purposes and one's theories-in-use.

CONCLUSION

I return to the quote with which this chapter began: "When teachers do not contextualize they tend to isolate various parts of a pedagogical circumstance and call each a problem" (Bohm & Edwards, 1991, as cited in Kincheloe, 2008, p. 33). Stated differently, when reflecting on classroom and school dynamics, one has to remain aware of the full range of forces in play. I find when it comes to the historical forces at play in schools, we are chillingly ignorant. Picture the cartoon of a swinging bridge of wooden slats over a gorge; as the character runs toward the other side of the gorge, the slats fall away behind him. So historical memory falls away behind us. Dan Lortie, in his classic work *Schoolteacher* (1975), refers to the "hand of history," citing, for example, the following: the origins of school funding through property taxes and a desire for local control; society's view of teachers as "special but shadowed," allowing us to think of teachers as doing something sacred but also of teaching as "easy"; or the rise of graded classrooms during the industrial revolution, built in the name of efficiency, like factories. Most important, the long arm of the history of slavery in this country, like the history of apartheid in South Africa, continues to leave its mark, like the imprint of a hand on a face that has been slapped, or much worse. As Dewey (1916) put it, the individual thinker must never see an event, or a person, as isolated, "but in its connection with the common experience of mankind" (pp. 342–343).

In reflecting on our practice, in being reflective teachers, we are obligated to consider each node of Hawkins's triangle, each axis of interaction, and all of the possible systemic forces at work before we judge ourselves, our students, or the world into which we are sending them.

REFLECTION

Why does reflection matter? For several reasons: because it provides a structure for thinking and a structure that disciplines thinking, which forces us to pause before acting. It forces us to gather evidence before jumping to conclusions. It slows us down to see a fuller story rather than acting from assumptions. It matters, especially now, to our democracy, to our relations with one another, to the lives of our children, to the health and survival of the planet. I know these are big claims, but we live in times that require communication and careful thinking that consider consequences.

What's reflection got to do with presence? The origins of my thinking about presence lie in my study of reflection. To teach reflectively is to be present. My understanding of reflection starts with the philosophy of John Dewey and extends to the work of others: Donald Schön's notions of reflection-in- and on-action (defined below); Paolo Freire's concept of praxis (reflection + action); and David Kolb's (1984) experiential learning cycle. Over the years, my understanding of the nature and complexity of reflection has deepened, but my notion of its basic structure remains consistent. I find the basic four-part flow—from experience, to description, to analysis and interpretation, to intelligent action[1]—to have stood the test of time, not just theoretically but in practice as well. I have not found a more effective or simpler way of doing it.

In this part, I delineate this flow, exploring its complexities and weaving in the elements of presence. In essence, I consider structured reflection-on-action (a slowed-down reflection done after action, looking back) to be training for reflection-in-action (thoughtful in-the-moment decisionmaking), the whole of which I equate with presence. Just as meditation is practice for being present and taking right action in the midst of life's lived moments, so structured reflection (reflection-*on*-action) is practice for awareness and right action in the midst of teaching (reflection-*in*-action). By "right action," I imply a moral foundation to both reflection and presence.

REFLECTION

CHAPTER 9

The Research

Much has been written about reflection in education, especially since the publication of Donald Schön's *The Reflective Practitioner* in 1983. But reflection itself is at least as old as the Greeks. I am not inventing anything new here. What is notable is that it has not gone the way of other trends in education. Virtually all teacher education programs claim to produce reflective practitioners, and no one would seek to hire an unreflective teacher. But views of reflection have varied depending on the research contexts of the time.

EARLY PROPONENTS

Reflection has been an integral ingredient in teacher education and professional development since the 1980s, following publication of *The Reflective Practitioner* (Schön, 1983), with backup from Dewey, particularly *How We Think* (1933). In addition, the advent of teacher action research in the early 1990s (spurred by Marilyn Cochran-Smith and Susan Lytle's book *Inside/ Outside* [1993]) and of professional learning communities in the early 2000s (e.g., DuFour & Eaker [1998]; Charlotte Danielson [2011]) has firmly established reflection as a foundation of good teaching. However, as modes of reflective practice have proliferated, a clear definition of reflection has faded, not because definitions haven't been clearly stated (see, for example, Zeichner & Liston's *Reflective Teaching: An Introduction* [1996]; Cochran-Smith & Lytle's *Inquiry as Stance* [2009]; Lyons's *Handbook of Reflection and Reflective Inquiry* [2010]; and my own article "Defining Reflection" [2002a]) but because the concept has been so widely and loosely applied that it has thinned and softened until now it means little more than thinking about "what went well, what didn't, and what should I do next time," especially in the minds of practicing teachers. For this it has earned its critics, and rightly so.

POSTSTRUCTURALIST CRITIQUE

Lynn Fendler, in her 2003 article "Reflection in a Hall of Mirrors," cites four influences on the notion of reflection: Cartesian epistemology, Dewey's *How*

We Think (1933), the work of Donald Schön (1983), and cultural feminism. From a Cartesian perspective, she argues, it is assumed that "self-awareness generates valid knowledge" (p. 17). This, according to Fendler, is a dangerous notion because it assumes we can make choices free and clear of the cultural and political forces that continuously shape us. Dewey's notion of reflection, she argues, needs to take account of the progressive times in which it was conceived, namely, a time of optimistic (and naïve) belief in progress committed to social betterment, where belief in conscious control over impulsive action through science and the scientific method was prevalent. In contrast to Descartes and Dewey's reasoned reflection, Schön's work on reflection-in-action illuminated an intuitive process of decisionmaking where the actor is in tacit dialogue with a situation, constantly revising action based on feedback from the situation (e.g., a teacher responding to the unpredictable events of the classroom). This vision of reflection as intuitive stands in tension with Dewey's notion of reflection and conscious control. Finally, Fendler declares that newer feminist approaches to reflection (e.g., Noddings, 1986; Richert, 1992) tend to rely on a notion of a "trustworthy inner self" that is exempt from the powers of socialization and dominant cultural norms (p. 20). "Such feminist accounts of reflectivity," Fendler argues,

> do not account for the fact that all ways of thinking and systems of reasoning—including reflective inquiry and communities of practice—are themselves products of historical power relations, and that there is no sure way to tell the difference between reflective thinking that is complicit with existing power hierarchies and reflective thinking that is authentic or innovative. (p. 20)

Coia and Taylor (2017) take Fendler's critique to heart and propose a poststructural feminist process of reflection that takes into account contextual powers to shape the reflective "self" (another contested notion). They insist that the very self who is reflecting also be an object of reflection in light of those powers. Coia and Taylor's process is rooted in self-study and "co-/autoethnography" involving an iterative, collaborative writing process aimed at unearthing various narratives of the self, which then become objects of reflection. They state the purpose of their reflection as promoting social justice with insight into the "ubiquity of power and its operation" (p. 54). They advocate a move away from technical, rational reflective "steps," and the courage to remain "in the swamp" of uncertainty that comes with teaching—Schön's reflection-in-action. And yet their process, although rich, takes an idiosyncratic written form and seems impractical when thinking about how teachers might organize to reflect together.

These critiques, as apt as they are, nonetheless leave us with not much of a leg to stand on in terms of ways to learn from practice. I take their shared warning that "if we do not maintain a skeptical and critical attitude about what we do, then we have little chance of discovering the ways our best intentions may be falling short of the mark" (Fendler, 2003, p. 23), but also believe that it is helpful to have a process that is practical, reliable, and replicable, although always open to skepticism and revision. This is what I feel my colleagues and I have developed over time.[2] While my understanding of the broad phases of the process has not changed since 2002, the complexity of each phase has deepened considerably, as has the content of reflection (I, Thou, It/Context).

DEWEY

Dewey had four criteria for reflection: that it is a meaning-making process that moves a learner from one experience into the next with deeper understanding of its relationships with and connections to other experiences and ideas; that it is a "systematic, rigorous, disciplined way of thinking, with its roots in scientific inquiry"; that it is a social process and must be done in the company of others; and that it requires particular attitudes, like open-mindedness, wholeheartedness, directness, responsibility, and curiosity (Rodgers, 2002a, p. 845).

What Dewey refers to is clearly a deliberative process that happens "outside" the action being reflected upon. Etymologically, it conveys the act of "bending back" (Latin: flectere, to bend, and re-, back). Its origins refer to light being "bent back" toward the viewer. In like fashion, reflection as I am describing it here aims at conjuring an image of what happened so that it can be thought about, not in the moment, but slowly, with time to consider its constituent elements and qualities. The world moves very fast, especially, perhaps, the world of the classroom. When reflecting, we call the classroom experience to mind—all of its parts, both visible and invisible: the people, physical environment and objects, the actions, and the energy associated with these—so that we can better "see" the situation.

But this is not what is generally meant by reflective teaching. Reflective teaching implies a particular *way of teaching* that is thoughtful, that considers the learner, the learning, the context, the subject matter, objectives, modes of entry and barriers, along with one's own motives in the act of teaching itself, in short, all elements of the I, Thou, and It/Context and their dynamics. It implies a teacher who not only thinks about her teaching, but thinks and feels—and is aware of these thoughts and feelings—*while* teaching. To use the words of mindfulness, she is someone who thoughtfully responds rather than reacts.

ADAPTIVE EXPERTISE

And yet teaching, not unlike racecar driving, skiing, basketball playing, jazz, or improv theater, requires dexterity and nimbleness—alert reactions—in response to rapidly changing, complex circumstances. Another term for this mode of responsiveness is *adaptive expertise*, a notion first conceived of by Japanese researchers Hatano and Inagaki (1986) in their work on children's learning. They posited that children developed two kinds of expertise—routine and adaptive. Both kinds of expertise depend upon an accumulation of experiences. Routine expertise, a craft-like notion of expertise, suggests mastery of particular ways of doing things in a fixed, predictable set of circumstances. It is procedural knowledge. By contrast, the notion of adaptive expertise suggests the capacity to adapt in-the-moment to unpredictable circumstances, which are viewed as an opportunity for a creative response to a new set of problems, drawing upon old knowledge, but also creating new knowledge in the process.

Teaching requires both routine and adaptive expertise. The countless number of ways that the variables in the classroom might come together (or blow up) make it nothing if not an "uncertain craft" (Lampert, 1985; McDonald, 1992) requiring adaptive expertise. On the other hand, this chaos is kept in check by predictable routines teachers work hard to establish in their classrooms: settling in, morning meetings, transitions from one activity to the next, hand signals, and so forth. However, an expert teacher, a creative and reflective teacher, could never remain at the level of routine. Those who do, usually engender boredom, if in not in their students, then in themselves. I would posit that reflection-on-action, which systematically explores all corners of the I, Thou, It/Context map, is a bridge between routine expertise and deft, adaptive expertise, something that looks like intuition, but is, in fact, the result of careful study.

Paradoxically, in the midst of the jazz-like act of teaching, there is also a slowing down, the capacity to see and make sense of complexity, and to choose what seems like the best response among many, that comes only with time and practice. This is the function of reflection-in-action. For example, if a student says, "He be mad," there are a number of ways teachers could respond. They could assume the student doesn't know what is correct English and give him the "correct" language; they could ask him to retrieve the correct language; they could ignore it, surmising that the situation called for dealing with something more important than language in that moment. They also could be aware of their privilege in having been raised to speak "proper English," and take stock of what a correction might mean in terms of the power dynamic; they could see the student's words as "correct" given the particular context; they could be explicit about this with the student, or fearful of pointing it out. Without reflection on the impact and possible implications of each of these choices, teachers act without awareness. With awareness, teachers can ask themselves what the situation calls for and begin a systematic process of testing actions, observing students' responses, watching their own internal dynamics, and beginning to learn from each—about teaching, about race, about privilege, about relationships, and so forth. Without reflection, all this remains implicit. And while teachers may be able to teach well from this tacit place, their opportunity to learn is lost; learning comes from awareness born of reflection (preferably with others) on experience.

You will recognize, in these descriptions of adaptive expertise and reflective teaching, presence. Reflective teaching *is* presence in teaching, and reflection-on-action is practice for reflective teaching. To wit, the sloweddown process of reflection-on-action is preparation for presence in teaching.

There is a moral vein that runs through reflection as well. If you have ever hiked the granite-lined White Mountains of New Hampshire or wandered along the craggy, grey, granite shores of Maine, you will have seen the white veins of quartz that run through them, intrusions that marble the granite, filling its gaps and cracks. Like these quartz veins, the moral imperative of reflection is inextricable from reflection itself and fills its gaps and cracks with purpose. This moral strain extends back to the purposes of education: Am I moving toward or away from what makes my students and myself more human and the world we live in more humane? More democratic? Maxine Greene put it this way: Can we, through reflection on our shared lives, imagine the world other than as "what it is," but as it might be? She writes:

> Once we can see our givens as contingencies, then we may have an opportunity to posit alternative ways of living and valuing and to make choices. . . . Social imagination is the capacity to invent visions of what should be and *what might be* in our deficit society, in the streets where we live and in our schools. Social imagination not only suggests but also requires that one take action to repair or renew. (1995, pp. 23, 5, emphasis in original)

CHAPTER 10

Purposes of Reflection

Below I offer a detailed picture of reflection as it has grown out of Dewey's work and developed in my own mind and practice over time. I begin with an overview of the purposes of reflection and follow this with a description of the four parts of reflection: experience, description, analysis and interpretation, and taking intelligent action.

I view the overarching purpose of reflection as closely wedded to my view of the purposes of education. Reflection alone is not an inherent good. It matters to what and whose ends we are reflecting in the first place.

I see four supporting purposes in practicing reflection: the development of perception, the development of acceptance of "what is," alignment of teaching practice with one's values, and alignment of practices with the purposes of education. I see all of these as moral practices. Overarching these is an attitude of inquiry and critique—where might I be wrong/doing harm/ perpetuating advantage or disadvantage?

THE DEVELOPMENT OF PERCEPTION

When I applied to graduate school, my statement of purpose articulated my desire to explore how teachers learn to "see." This is still a driving question of mine. By "see," I meant, literally, *to see.* By way of example, I offer the story of a teacher I once supervised; I'll call him Marcus. Marcus had graduated from an ivy league school and was exceedingly articulate and intellectually insightful. He had written some stunning papers during the fall semester and seemed to have a solid understanding of what it meant to have learning guide teaching. His internship was in a large city in Spain where he taught evening classes to a group of 2nd-graders and another group of teenaged girls.

He taught the 2nd-graders in a primary school after school hours, in a building that was otherwise empty at that time of day. The floors were made of marble; the desks and chairs were metal with no pads on their feet. There was nothing on the plaster walls, and sound was magnified and echoed by the emptiness.

One afternoon when I was there 20 children entered the room like a weather system. They had just come from a birthday party and were loaded down with hard candies and balloons. They haphazardly (loudly) took their seats, most of them with screams of post-birthday delight. Into the din, without pausing to check in with the students, or waiting for them to settle, Marcus began to teach. I do not recall what he was teaching, and I'm quite sure the children had no idea. He just started talking. Aware that he was paying them no mind, the children scraped back their chairs and desks, threw a candy or two or 20, and like a swarm started buzzing around the room. They took to blowing up their balloons and releasing the air, balloons held to their backsides—20 delighted children, balloon-farting and screeching with joy. I feebly tried to get them to sit down—this was Marcus's show, after all—but doing so was more like playing whack-a-mole than helping.

After class (I was exhausted) I asked Marcus my standard supervisory question: "What did you notice?" He said, "Nothing in particular."

"Huh. Did you see the kids getting out of their seats? Hear the noise?"

"Not really." How was this possible, I wondered? How can you be in front of 20 whooping, candy-throwing children running around making rude noises with brightly colored balloons, scraping metal across marble, and not notice? But there it was; he could take in only what he attended to (recall Kahneman's rule, "What you see is all there is"), and he was attending to his lesson, not to his students. In order to respond in ways that would bring students' attention to what Marcus intended for them to learn, he first had to see the reality of what was going on in front of him.

Another example of seeing (and not seeing) can be found in the now-famous invisible gorilla video.[3] (If you have not seen it, you might want to watch it now before reading further.) There are six players, three in white and three in black tee-shirts, passing a basketball and moving around, slowly, in front of three closed sets of elevator doors. In the video, developed by researchers Daniel Simons and Christopher Chabris (1999), viewers are asked to count the number of times the players wearing white pass the basketball to one another. In the midst of their throwing the ball to one another, a gorilla (a man dressed in a gorilla suit) enters from the right, walks slowly across the court, through the players, stops briefly to beat his chest, and then exits the scene on the left. After a couple of minutes the video stops, and viewers are asked the number of passes they saw. The voice on the video gives the correct answer (15) and continues, "But did you see the gorilla?!"

When I have shown this to my students, usually more than half have missed the gorilla altogether and are incredulous. They demand to see the video again and are equally incredulous that they could have missed it. Simons, in a TEDx talk (2011), makes the case that "what you actually experience is what your mind and your brain give you—it's an alternate reality." He notes that the power of the mind's intuition for what "should" happen in any given situation is so strong that when something aberrant (like a gorilla) shows up, our minds don't take it in. Marcus was not looking for flying candy or listening for balloon farts, and he was not expecting students to be running around while he was talking, so he didn't see them. His attention was narrowly focused on his own words and actions and plans, and ignorant of theirs.

Later, watching Marcus teach his teenagers, I saw a different kind of misperception. Students were polite and cooperative, but there was no connection between teacher and students. It was as though the wires had gone dead. David Hawkins (1974/2002) writes of students who have learned to "rather passively [sit] in neat rows and columns and [manipulate] you into believing that they're being attentive because they're not making any trouble" (p. 57). They allow you to teach, but because they are passive and disconnected, there is not much to see. Without much to go by, teaching becomes "just teaching," and not a response to learning. When Marcus and I spoke about it afterward, I suggested he get to know his students better, using activities that related more to them and their lives. I later discovered that he was taking his students—young teenaged girls—out to bars one-by-one "to get to know them." Not precisely what I'd had in mind. His perception of the situation was focused less on the students and their learning than on the convention of how you "get to know someone." You go out for a drink.

Marcus is, of course, an extreme example; all teachers must learn, and are always learning, how to see, although some come better equipped than others to notice patterns, signs of understanding and misunderstanding, indications of unease, boredom, interest. In a fascinating essay entitled "To See and Not See," Oliver Sacks (1995) reminds us that no one is born knowing how to see, knowing how to read the world. Sacks points out that we all must learn how to make sense of color, shadow, pattern, movement, line. He tells the story of Virgil, a man rendered blind by cataracts caused by a severe illness at the age of 3. At age 40, Virgil had an operation to remove the cataracts and return his sight to him. At the unwinding of the bandages, his wife and doctor stood by expectant and excited that Virgil would be able "to see" again. But what Virgil "saw" was nothing more than light and shadow, incoherent forms, and color. A "face" was not construed as a face. There was no perception of distance or proximity, no meaning in the visible phenomena. Sacks writes, "When we [who are sighted from birth] open our eyes each morning, it is upon a world we have spent a lifetime learning to see. We are not given the world: we make our world through incessant experience, categorization, memory, reconnection. . . . [Virgil] saw, but what he saw had no coherence" (p. 114).

So, not only do teachers need to learn to actually take in information; they also need to learn, "through incessant experience, categorization, memory, reconnection" (reflection), to make meaning of it. This is where teachers (or mentors or parents) help by putting language to phenomena, speeding along the learning process. Reflection plays the same function—putting language to experience, or naming the world. By ordering experiential phenomena into categories, noting patterns, we have easier access to meaning and, thus, mobility through mountains of otherwise disconnected information. We are able to "[construct] interpretations and meanings at ever higher levels" (Sacks, 2019, p. 153). It is an evolving, outwardly spiraling process, encompassing more and more of the world. Occasionally meaning also collapses completely with the introduction of new frames and has to be reorganized and reconstructed.

So, development of perception, refined by reflection, enables us both to see more and to make more complex meanings of what we see, which in turn supports more intelligent, more compassionate action in response. It takes a commitment to a stance of not knowing, of inquiry. This is long-term work, best done with others.

ACCEPTING WHAT IS

Presence and reflection include the ability not just to perceive what is but to accept what one sees without pushing it away. The students you teach can be only where they are in their learning. They can't know more than they know in that moment. They know what they know; they feel what they feel. What choice do we have but to begin there? All the frustration in the world on our part does not change "what is" for them. It can be understandably difficult for teachers to accept where their students are, with so much "stuff" to cover. They can see students as slowing things down, as apathetic, or as "fine" (when they're not) because getting through is what so often seems to matter. Starting from where students are means accepting the truth of where they are.

ALIGNMENT OF PRACTICES WITH SELF

The third purpose of reflection is the alignment of one's practices with one's self. Put another way, am I teaching what I value? Am I teaching from my self?

In 6th grade my son, Jon, had an English teacher (whose actual name was Mrs. Shakespeare) whom he loved. As often happens with a good teacher, she was snatched out of the classroom to fill a suddenly vacant administrative position and was replaced by another teacher, kind and generous but with little experience or subject matter knowledge. I asked Jon one day how she was doing. His response was, "Well, she's really nice and can control the kids but she teaches too much from the book and not enough from her *self*." I took this to mean that she had not internalized the subject matter or made it a part of herself. It lay outside herself, in a book, unintegrated. She was, in a sense, "beside herself."

A second example of alignment (or lack thereof) between practice and self comes from beginning teachers who speak of their "teacher selves" and their "real selves." They have a notion of how they "should" be in the classroom. The specter of tenure directs them toward a list of behaviors and a self that does not necessarily align with who they are. The burden of lugging around this other self, trying to fit into its skin, while simultaneously denying the self that, when at ease, can shine, is a heavy one. It can lead to burnout or, worse, cynicism.

In his trilogy for young adults, *His Dark Materials*,[4] Philip Pullman (1996) creates a world where each person is born with a "daemon." Daemons are animals that are the external manifestations of a person's "true self" or soul. In childhood these daemons constantly change shape until, in adolescence, they "settle." They are the constant companions of their humans, always close, never more than a few feet away. If daemons are ever too far from their humans, it causes a searing pain—separation. One of the most painful parts of Pullman's story is when the antagonist, Mrs. Coulter, kidnaps children and, with a cutting machine, cruelly severs the connection between the children and their daemons, a procedure Pullman calls "intercision."

In like fashion, the "intercision" of the personal from the professional self, caused by impersonal systems, can be dehumanizing. If the separation is too painful (or numbing), it is nearly impossible to be present. Teachers' contexts can either welcome and support their wholeness or undermine it. If there is alignment between the values one holds and the values the institution embodies (which are not always aligned with an institution's publicly espoused values), presence is certainly easier. Nonetheless, many, many teachers work in contexts that don't align with their own values.

There are two things to say here, I think. One references the work that teachers must do with themselves, which I will get to in a moment. The other concerns institutional presence. Just as teachers need to be present to students and their learning, schools—that is, the people who make the decisions about professional development, promotion to tenure, and supervision—need to be present to teachers and their professional–personal selves and consciously work not to be instruments of "intercision."

But exhorting schools to be more supportive goes only so far. Teachers also must work to be present to themselves. In her essay "Poiesis," Margaret Himley (Himley, 2010) explores the concept of "ethical self-making" and the idea that the individual has the capacity and responsibility to choose how to respond to institutional and societal norms. What scares Himley is

> the ease with which we become agents of norms. The insidious and everyday ways that norms capture us, fasten us all too securely within them, squelch our aesthetic and ethical desire to be a certain kind of person, and cause us to disavow our capacity for finding our baseline and making a difference. (p. 151)

Instead, Himley, like Maxine Greene (below) and many other philosophers before them, advocates not succumbing, but "crafting a relation to an unchosen world" and authoring a self that resists. As Greene writes in *Landscapes of Learning* (1978), reality is interpreted and it is our moral responsibility to shape it.

> I am suggesting that, for too many individuals in modern society, there is a feeling of being dominated and that feelings of powerlessness are almost inescapable. I am also suggesting that such feelings can to a large degree be overcome through conscious endeavor on the part of individuals to keep themselves awake, to think about their condition in the world, to inquire into the forces that appear to dominate them, to interpret the experiences they are having day by day. Only as they learn to make sense of what is happening, can they feel themselves to be autonomous. Only then can they develop the sense of agency required for living a moral life. (p. 44)

My point is that there is a self (albeit an always evolving, shifting self) that comes into the classroom. When you can bring your best self with you, and that self is supported, it feels wonderful and everyone benefits. When that self is violated by requirements, schedules, tests, bullet lists, and so forth, it can be oppressive. It matters to seek the kind of alignment between self and practice that frees rather than oppresses that self. In addition, that same self is incomplete, with perennial room for growth; there are parts of the self that aren't pretty. Unless the self is consciously and intentionally examined, one risks teaching from some ugly and unconscious "theories-in-use."[5] If I preach differentiation in teaching, do my students experience it? Have I asked them? Does their experience align with my perceptions of it? If I stand against racism and gender discrimination, does my teaching align with this stance? Do I analyze my practice through these lenses? What am I not seeing? How will I get that information? I believe seeking this kind of alignment is what is meant by integrity. It involves denying those jaded voices that say, "You'll never be able to teach that way here," or the inner voice that worries, "I can't teach that way until I get tenure." I speak here to idealistic beginning teachers especially, urging you to hold onto those ideals, to find allies, and bring them to life.

ALIGNMENT OF PRACTICES WITH THE PURPOSES OF EDUCATION

There are, for me, three large purposes of education, which I have already discussed: to support and extend one's humanness, to be a contributing member of our democracy, and to contribute to the health of the planet. I won't repeat the discussion here except to say that the current educational world focuses almost exclusively on making education a commodity where teachers and students must produce "results." In the United States, we must measure up, succeed, and compete with one another and other countries in order to be "first" (we're not). We are urged to be productive and efficient. This is exhausting for everyone.

It falls directly upon teachers, then, to resist (although not ignore) this imposed focus. Reflection, both with other teachers and with one's students, makes space for inquiry into big questions of what makes us human, what is necessary for our growth, what is moral and just. Maxine Greene, in her 1977 essay "Wide-Awakeness and the Moral Life," writes, "We are all aware how few people ask themselves what they have done with their own lives, whether or not they have used their freedom or simply acceded to the imposition of patterned behavior and the assignment of roles" (n.p.). How do we support the development of the kind of agency that the students of Marjory Stoneman Douglas High School in Parkland, Florida, exhibited after the horrific school shootings there? Or Greta Thunberg and the thousands of children who marched as part of the youth climate movement? They are all outraged that we have paid so little attention to what matters. So, the fourth purpose of reflection is to remember what matters, and to make sure that we are spending our time and our students' time on that.

CHAPTER 11

The Process of Reflection

The structure of reflection, which, as Dewey described it and as I've interpreted it, moves through four phases: from experience, to description, to analysis and interpretation, to taking intelligent action. It does not differ from teacher to student. It is the same process. What does differ from student to teacher is the focus of their reflection. For students, it is on the subject matter and/or on their experience learning the subject matter. For teachers, it is both this and the implications for their teaching. For teacher educators or mentors, it involves yet another layer—they will reflect on their teaching, teachers' learning of teaching, and students' learning of the subject matter. For those of us who study teacher education, it is on all four levels: subject matter, student, teacher, teacher educator. Each level is nested within the next (see Figure 11.1). The focus is different and more encompassing for each party, but the process is the same.

The process of reflection can happen over time or in a moment. Logically, *after* one experience is the same thing as *before* the next experience, so reflection is also a looking forward and a part of planning. Finally, it can happen alone or with others, but Dewey believed that it is an incomplete process if done alone.

When I introduce reflection to teachers, they sometimes will say that, yes, they give students a survey at the beginning or end of a course, or that as student-teachers they wrote in their journals about what worked and what didn't and what they would do differently. I would argue that reflection is neither a survey of students nor a journal entry. These are data, but they must be contextualized, analyzed, checked against purposes, and rendered meaningful in some way. The process of reflection is spiral-like. It is both iterative, in that one moves back and forth between the four phases, and linear, in that although circular in nature, it is also ever-widening and forward moving (see Figure 11.2). It is more a spiral than a circle. I explore each phase below. Reflection is usually thought of only in terms of teaching. But reflection is a way of thinking and thus applies both to students learning subject matter and teachers learning teaching. Nonetheless, in an effort to avoid confusion, I speak here only of teacher reflection. Later, in Part V, I give several examples of students' experiences of reflection.

A process note: When working with teachers, it is important to head off the deeply engrained habits of advice-giving and problem solving until the

Figure 11.1. The Nested Nature of Reflection

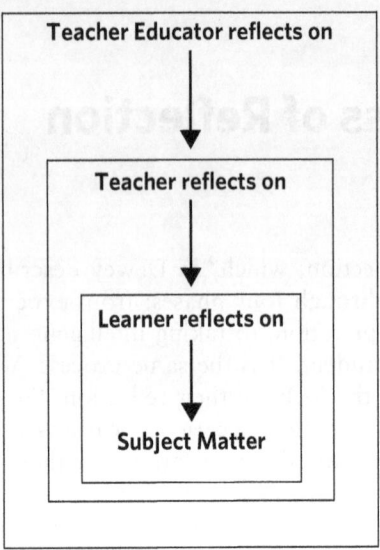

Figure 11.2. Process of Reflection

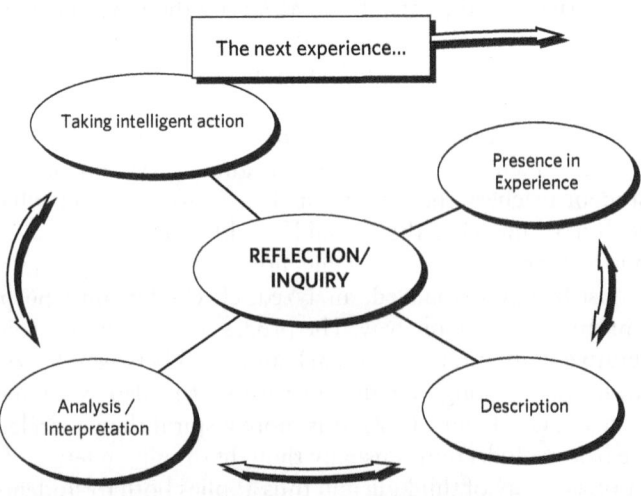

very end of the process. To this end, it is useful to have three things in place: a negotiated set of norms that includes no advice-giving, a clear picture of the reflective process they are following, and a skilled facilitator willing to hold teachers to the process.

PHASE 1: EXPERIENCE

Dewey (1938) makes it clear that all learning begins with an experience. He defines experience in the following way. An educative experience is composed of two qualities: interaction and continuity. Interaction signifies engagement by the learner (and by learner, I include the teacher-learner) with the environment.

> An experience is always what it is because of a transaction taking place between an individual and what, at the time, constitutes his environment, whether the latter consists of persons with whom he is talking about some topic or event, the subject talked about being also a part of the situation; or the toys with which he is playing; the book he is reading; . . . or the materials of an experiment he is performing. (p. 44)

Continuity, the second aspect of an educative experience, points to the principle that every learning experience builds upon past experiences and carries over to subsequent experience. Continuity connotes direction and growth. The principle of continuity is embodied in the idea of a curriculum. Each piece of a curriculum is designed to build on previous pieces and lead one outward to a greater understanding of the subject in question. My own way of understanding the relationship between continuity and interaction is through the analogy of a river and its banks. Think of students as the river and the teacher as the banks of the river. The banks of a river, which also includes the curriculum or course of study (like the course of a river), keep the river moving in a direction. Although the banks determine the shape of its journey and its destination, it is the river that moves under its own power. But those banks are also made of earth (unless it's the Los Angeles River) and as such not only shape the river but are also shaped by it. The banks and the river's direction undergo constant shifts under the force of the river (as well as other environmental forces). As the river moves towards the ocean, it takes pieces of the banks and riverbed with it. Each, in their interaction, is changed by the other.

So an experience is what the teacher sets up—the activity plan and its constituent parts, as well as the end-in-view. But once set up, it belongs to the students. The teacher's job then is to observe, intervening (which is different from interfering) with the right question, idea, or fact when students show signs of not being able to go further under their own power. When it comes time for the teacher to reflect, there must be an experience to reflect upon. The more interaction there has been, the more there is to see and reflect upon.

PHASE 2: DESCRIPTION

We learn to see a thing by learning to describe it.

—Raymond Williams (1961), as cited in Himley, 2000, p. vi

The second phase of reflection is description of experience. In many ways, I view it as the heart of reflection. It is the phase that teaches me to slow down and take in what is there to perceive before reacting to what I think happened/is happening. It helps me to see more than what I thought I saw and to fend off actions based on thin slices of evidence. It is a discipline that trains me to pause before acting or jumping to conclusions.

The teacher can describe her experience with students, their learning, and their work, as well as her own responses to all these. In addition, there exist the contextual factors, both visible and invisible, to be described. Finally, there are the teacher's own inner actions (feelings, emotions, thoughts) to be described. All of these are contained in the I, Thou, It/Contexts map.

The most useful question I have found in eliciting description is, "What do/did you notice?" It is a question that comes before "What does X mean?" or, "What went well, what didn't, and why?" When a teacher looks at herself on video and berates her looks, points out all the things she did wrong, and judges herself as inadequate, she has missed seeing both her teaching and herself whole. In the press of the highly scheduled world of school, we have equated efficiency with speed, and, like driving through the landscape instead of walking, we may get to where we're going faster, but we've missed so much along the way.

There are a number of techniques available for practicing the skill of description, many of which are delineated in Part V. But I offer one example here by way of illustration. When I work with groups of teachers reflecting on their teaching, they almost always begin by evaluating and judging themselves and how they have taught (especially when video is involved), or they deflect, judging their students or the "system." As I noted above, it is vital that a skilled facilitator remind teachers that, at this phase, they are only gathering evidence and not offering advice or solutions. The I, Thou, and It/Context map also can be useful in reminding teachers what there is to describe.

Below I describe a group of teachers looking at a videotape of their teaching. They are a small group of high school math, science, and ESL teachers collaborating to make their content more accessible to their immigrant and refugee students. As they watch the video-recording of the lesson, their instruction is to fill out a sheet of paper with three columns labeled "What the teacher did," "What the students did," and "Clarifying questions." When the tape selection is over, they share their noticings. If a teacher "notices" that a student is "uncomfortable," I ask the teacher (and they ask one another) where in the recording they saw that and to describe what suggests discomfort. I also ask, "What else could it suggest?" Eventually the weight of the evidence points to one or two particular interpretations that seem reliable. One teacher, looking at a small group with one immigrant student, concludes that the student doesn't understand. "How do you know? What tells you that?" "They aren't saying anything. They're lost." "What else could be going on?" I ask. The group offers multiple interpretations, from unfamiliarity with vocabulary and context, to deep familiarity with the subject matter, which also might result in nonparticipation. At this point, they are moving between the phases of description and analysis/interpretation (which is why the arrows in Figure 11.2 go in both directions). Finally, in the last phase of reflection (intelligent action), they formulate a plan to interview ESL students to find out what kinds of math and science skills they are bringing with them, not just from school, but from their home lives. These interviews in turn lead to a reworking of math problems that includes mining some of the students' "funds of knowledge,"[6] which include participating in their families' business, managing money, political and geographical knowledge—whatever knowledge they carry with them.

In addition to describing what they see, it is also important for teachers to describe their own internal responses and to hold those up to scrutiny as well. For example, if a teacher is fearful of embarrassing a student or making the student uncomfortable by asking for clarification, on what basis is that feeling founded? Is it justified by the evidence? What assumptions are being made about the student's fragility or strength, about the cultural memes in play, and so forth? While any interpretation is always tentative and in need of testing, this process makes room for awareness to grow.

As noted in Phase 1, Experience, one of the most compelling aspects of description is that teachers begin to realize that certain ways of structuring curriculum, activities, and the physical classroom itself offer more opportunities to observe learning than others. Those who only lecture, those who spend most of their time "telling," and those who have a poorly organized or chaotic structure have descriptions that are far less robust than those who create opportunities for observation of students' experiments, constructions, and mistakes. When teachers create opportunities to observe students' learning, they begin to perceive nuance, detail, and tone—fuchsias, golds, and azures instead of blocks of primary colors.

PHASE 3: ANALYSIS AND INTERPRETATION[7]

French polymath and philosopher of science Henri Poincaré (1854–1912) wrote, "Science is built up with facts, as a house is with stones. But a collection of facts is no more a science than a heap of stones is a house" (1904, n.p.). While "facts" might be a strong term for the elements described in the complex and ever-emerging context of the classroom, the point is well-taken. Some sense has to be made of the data that have been gathered through description.

I view analysis as a process of sorting the pieces of gathered experience, a sort of taking stock—asking: What have we got here? What different "houses" can we build from these stones? Which house seems the most stable? Which are most amenable to additions and alterations in the future? (Of course, at some point this same house may need to be bulldozed and a totally new one built.)

Interpretation is the process of meaning-making, where a number of different explanations for, or "conjectures" (Lampert & Ball, 1999) about what the description suggests, are considered. Eventually a tentative theory or hypothesis is settled upon, which one is willing to test in action. As mentioned above, although analysis and interpretation come after description, there is often a dialectical, give-and-take relationship between these two phases. During this third phase, it is often necessary to return to the descriptive phase and seek more data, which in turn may point toward different analyses.

Below I relate one case of teachers moving between description and analysis and interpretation, to arrive at a deeper understanding of an artifact. It will be plain that the process is hard to neatly divide into description on one hand, and analysis/interpretation[8] on the other. It is a dialectical process.

Grounding Analysis in the Text of Experience

A number of years ago I was a professional development consultant at a small, progressive public school in southern Vermont. The majority of our work involved describing and analyzing/interpreting a single artifact: one sheet of paper on which School Rules were listed. Teachers and students had developed the list some years prior; since that time there had been some faculty turnover and "old" faculty were invested in newer faculty understanding some of the history of the school and its values. In an effort to immerse ourselves in this history and the principles that made up the school's identity, the faculty, including the relatively new principal, decided to look at this particular artifact, which embodied this history, the school's principles, and a piece of its identity. I think of artifacts as elements of an "experience" in that there is interaction between them and the "reader" of the artifact.

We first tilled the ground for reflection by telling stories from the early days of the school, watching a movie a local filmmaker had made about its first principal, and reflecting together on the word *home*.[9] Often a focusing question accompanies an inquiry.[10] Our question was, "How do we know when we're home?" We then read the School Rules aloud and got our first impressions off our chests. These impressions included, "The safety rules seem to be met inconsistently," "We have rules about things that in other places would be against the rules," and "The rules demand a great deal of responsibility on the part of the students." From there we backed up to read carefully through each rule, describing what it was saying. (When I say "describing" in reference to something in writing, I mean paraphrasing it, but sticking very close to the original meaning, almost like translating it into different English. This is different from glossing or offering a superficial summary of the text.) Three months later (meeting every other week) we were still only on the second rule! And the first rule was only five words long: "No running in the halls." As we attempted to describe the rule, we immediately got involved in determining what actually was meant by "no running" and by "running" itself. Did no running mean no running ever? Teachers recognized that *they* ran—did this rule apply just to students? And what qualified as running, anyway? In an attempt to describe, we found ourselves interpreting. So teachers went back to what they'd observed for more evidence. What about the basketball lay-up move the junior high kids did? Did that count as running? Was dancing running? What about going up or down the stairs two at a time? This discussion led to an analysis of the nature of a rule. What did it mean to enforce a rule? Did it apply 100% of the time? Always in the same way? The group also noted that parents were players in the whole question of rules and often were called upon to reinforce adherence to them.

Over the weeks, the discussion evolved into one about why rules exist in the first place. We determined that rules were guidelines for behavior but not necessarily what teachers wanted students to learn. What the teachers really valued was not, strictly speaking, "students obeying the rules" (being obedient children), but students paying attention to the space between us, that is, becoming aware that their actions have an impact on others, even those who aren't present at the time, not only in school but in life. Other values included safety, school stewardship, and taking responsibility for one's own actions. As we contemplated the nature of rules, the faculty also affirmed its appreciation of the value of freedom for their kids. This prompted me to bring in Dewey's short chapter on "The Nature of Freedom"[11] from *Experience and Education* (1938). We spent a 2-hour session describing one sentence of the chapter: "The ideal aim of education is creation of the power of self-control" (p. 75). The group determined that the "power of self-control" was distinct from "self-control" alone, since it focused on students' *power* of self-determination rather than on their ability to control themselves—to "be good." This in turn led to deeper insight about the kind of learning that the teachers wanted to nurture in their students—about helping them find within themselves that power of self-determination, with the concomitant attention to and care for those with whom they interacted. Following this weeks-long process, the faculty renamed the School Rules, "School Rules, Recess Rules, and Life Rules."

Now, nearly 20 years later, I am still moved by the stunning complexity and depth hidden beneath the simple surface of these rules. While the process was slow in terms of the rules we "covered," the depth of understanding that emerged from the iterative processes of description and analysis/interpretation was, I felt, durable. Yes, it took time, but in the end, it not only saved time, but allowed teachers to enforce the rules by the spirit of the law, rather than by the letter of the law, with a finely tuned sense of the rule's intent, and with integrity. I recently contacted two teachers who were a part of that process of 20 years ago. While they do not refer to the rules per se, they tell me that our process—taking a "deep dive" into questions—found its way into their work with kids. They took time to explore things deeply through something they called "fieldwork," getting to know their community in depth, and coming to feel a part of it. This kind of reflection leads to owning the knowledge that emerges, what today might be called "deep learning."

Developing a Common Analytical Language

Relatedly, there is a need for teachers, and learners, to generate a common language about teaching and learning. In the process of turning over evidence and asking what is going on, I frequently run into words that seem to carry shared meaning, but when we scratch the surface of the word, different meanings emerge. A word like *engagement* may hold multiple meanings for the teachers around the table and for students. What does it mean to be engaged in the first place? Have fun? Stay on task? Does it necessarily include learning? Is engagement enough? *Learning* is another of these words. While there is as yet no common language across education, there can be a common language within a community of inquiry. Teachers and facilitators need to assume the responsibility of asking one another and their students to define what they mean by words or terms that we assume are commonly understood.

Such reflective work allows one to direct the course of similar future experiences and leads toward "intelligent action." But Dewey also would caution that the meaning we make is always tentative and open to revision.

PHASE 4: TAKING INTELLIGENT ACTION
(BECAUSE AWARENESS IS NOT ENOUGH)

Because any conclusions drawn from analysis and interpretation are tentative, every action taken based on them is also an experiment. It may or may not be the right action for that particular problem, or it may be that what might have worked in the first instance will not work the next time a similar problem occurs. Still, we can't be paralyzed by the inherent unpredictability of the classroom. A teacher has to act—a thousand times a day; but the chances of acting in a more productive, moral, compassionate, and kind way are better if we've taken the time to pause and consider the human elements in play as well as those contextual forces that shape our behavior.

Again, to try to ground this rather abstract discussion of reflection in a concrete example, let's look at the math and science teachers sharing a problem of practice concerning their non-native students. As already mentioned the math and science teachers generated a number of ideas (not advice) for ways to make their content more accessible to their non-native speakers. Along with deciding to interview students and mine some of their funds of knowledge, teachers also decided to experiment with using gestures and pictures, facing the class rather than the board when giving directions, and giving students opportunities to express their thinking and to make it visible—to speak, to draw, to create a skit, to construct a project.

It is important to remember that experiments often do not work the first time! They need to go through adjustments and refinements and should not be abandoned out of hand. Intelligent action becomes the next experience (a word which shares the same root as "experiment," and in French, is the same exact word) to reflect upon, and the cycle, for both teacher and students, continues—forever.

SUMMARY

I return to the question posed at the start of this chapter: What does reflection have to do with presence in teaching? If we define presence as "a state of alert awareness, receptivity, and connectedness to the mental, emotional, and physical workings of both the individual and the group in the context of their learning environments, and the ability to respond with a considered and compassionate best next step" (Rodgers & Raider-Roth, 2006, p. 266), reflection serves several purposes. It cultivates awareness by asking teachers and students to look closely at what *is*. It does not ask them to see everything, because that is impossible, but it does ask them to slow down to see what there is to see with one another's help. It engenders a receptivity to or acceptance of "what is" because responding to anything else is beside the point. If it becomes clear that students are not learning, to move blithely on to the next chapter for the sake of finishing, seems, at least to me, like a waste of everyone's time. If one must "move on," at least one (teacher or student) should be aware of what (and who) is being foregone, and to whose ends. Are students being left "just at the bottom" while others are "all the way up here," as Bettina described it, and what are the consequences of that? By reflecting, a teacher is put in connection with students, colleagues, and herself, as well as the subject matter and the contextual forces in play. The same goes for the students, who are put in touch with the subject matter, fellow learners, and the teacher, as well as themselves. This connection makes room for further learning, as well as responding to one another with compassion.

When students are asked to reflect with teachers on the teaching-learning project in which they are both engaged, describing their learning, offering suggestions about what would best serve their learning next, they become wonderfully imaginative partners in the experiment that is teaching. (I'll have more to say about this in Part V in my discussion of description feedback.) At the same time they may develop compassion for the teacher, whose job it is to serve them as well as to serve a system—a system that, together, they can interrogate and, possibly (ahem), subvert.

CHAPTER 12

Reflective Practice, Mindful Practice, and Presence in Teaching

For many years, my colleagues Claire Stanley and Jack Millet,[12] both teacher educators and teachers of mindfulness practice, and I have had ongoing discussions about the convergences and divergences between reflective and mindfulness practices. I think that presence in teaching lies at the intersection of the two.

Both reflection and mindfulness practices are more than mere techniques, even though each can be used as such. Both practices have been reduced in some cases to tools by a marketplace that promises efficiency, effectiveness, and success as a result. Mindfulness as a commodity has become big business. (Once I even saw a mindful salad listed on a menu.) Large corporations like Google have developed executive training programs (Google's is called Search Inside Yourself), which claim to cultivate mindfulness, emotional intelligence, and compassionate leadership at work in order to gain a marketing edge. The military has developed mindfulness-based fitness training, and mindfulness programs in schools promise to reduce fights, outbursts, and suspensions, and improve test results. In my own town a mindfulness organization promises personal success.

Likewise, reflection is tacked onto almost all teacher education programs, and most states write reflective practice into their standards for teachers. This often has translated into perfunctory practices like keeping journals. The focus is generally on the goodness or badness of what the teacher has done rather than on teaching as a response to students' learning. In the meantime, professional development programs like Critical Friends, the Danielson Framework, and commercial communities of practice like the Dufour program have proliferated, been sold to states, and become big business.

All this notwithstanding, what reflection and mindfulness have in common, when they are seen not as mere programs and techniques, but as processes of inquiry, is an inquiry stance with a moral core. Carini (2001) reminds us that "the subject of my attention always exceeds what I can see. . . . I learn that when I see a lot, I am still seeing only a little and partially" (p. 163). Reflection and mindfulness both start with openness, with not knowing, or with provisional knowing. Far be it from me to define the purpose of mindfulness, but I know it is not to be a fitter, more successful, more efficient worker. I do know that it aims at being a more compassionate human being. As with mindfulness, the practice of reflection has a purpose beyond the practitioner herself. The point is to see, accept what one sees, understand what one sees, and respond in a compassionate way that best serves the learner and the world in which the learner and teacher both live. In a word, to be present. To be present in teaching is to take a moral stance of inquiry. It is also a philosophical stance, one, to invoke Carini again (2010), without which "we suffer the pain of being without anchor, adrift, bereft, a plaything of fate" (p. 156).

A distinction that might be made between meditation practice and reflection is that the former tends to be an individual practice (although often done in community, it is done in silence), while the latter is best done in a community of practice (by talking with others). Dewey was emphatic that reflection done solely at the individual level was incomplete. He believed that a thought unexpressed to others was a thought unfinished. Having a sense of something is different from putting it into words to another, and it is often in putting it into words that we learn what it is that we are thinking. Further, he believed that for others to have access to one's sense-making, it has to be communicated. When we communicate our own experience, we also are forced to imagine how another might hear it. This asks us to imagine how another's experience might connect with ours. If we lived solitary rather than communal lives, we would not, Dewey (1916) says, be required to reflect: "A [person] really living alone (alone mentally as well as physically) would have little or no occasion to reflect upon his past experience to extract its net meaning" (p. 6).

I would venture to say that where reflection moves outward, making sense with others, meditation moves inward. Through contemplation on oneself, one's motivations, one's actions, one's thoughts, one's impact on others, one moves toward "clear comprehension" with an awareness of the purpose and appropriateness of what one is doing. Joseph Goldstein (2013) writes that "as we settle into a growing awareness of ourselves, we begin to realize that our practice is not for ourselves alone, but can be for the benefit and happiness of all beings" (p. 12).

I think that teaching reflectively and teaching mindfully are more or less the same. It is the getting there that differs. Like meditation, reflection moves toward an in-the-moment awareness, with moral purpose: acting with kindness, extending one's own humanness and that of others—simply put, making the world a better place.[13] Presence grows out of both practices, and perhaps more so out of both practiced in tandem.

Part V

EDUCATING FOR PRESENCE: HOW DO WE LEARN TO BE PRESENT? HOW CAN IT BE TAUGHT?

The purpose of this part, meant to be practical, is to provide examples of how teachers might be educated for presence. I provide assignments, examples of student work, and lists of readings, as well as reflections on how each module connects to the cultivation of reflection and presence. I hope that teachers and teacher educators will use it, modify and expand upon it, and share with me and others how their efforts have unfolded.[1]

Since the year 2000, I have taught a master's level course to new and experienced teachers called "Understanding Learning and Teaching." The purpose of the course is to introduce teachers to reflective teaching by taking them through all parts of the reflective cycle (as outlined in Part IV), but with a special emphasis on description. It is a course designed to force teachers to slow down, to *see*, and to respond to learners and their learning. While this part is directed primarily at teacher educators, teachers also can "try the exercises and readings at home," either on their own or with others.

For the first 10 years this course[2] was taught face-to-face. Then, as the lives of our students grew busier and more complex, the demand for online offerings increased. With great reluctance I switched from face-to-face teaching to a text-based online format. I was very worried that I would be giving up what I loved about teaching: experiential activities, human contact, community, dialogue, laughter and spontaneity, sharing food, and possibilities for presence. While I did have to give up some of these (food and spontaneity), I discovered, to my great surprise, that most of this was not only possible, but in many cases enhanced. In fact, I was able to be *more* present than in face-to-face classes. In the online environment, I was able to see each student in ways that were impossible face-to-face. Imagine 25 students, each a page in a stack of 25 stories, each page with different words and pictures. In a face-to-face class, when I am talking, those pages are stacked in one pile—I can get a sense of the "stack" but I don't see more than its edges. Even when I put them into small groups (stacks of five pages, if you will), and students are doing the talking, I still can see only one or two at a time. Rarely, if ever, do I see all 25. But in an online environment, especially one that is primarily text-based, it is as though the pages are spread out on the table in front of me. I see each one, its words and colors (always changing like something from a Harry Potter book), and the time I spend with each one is not bounded by 3-hour blocks. Each student is read, and I have the time to truly respond, or to reread and reword my more hasty responses. The egalitarian nature of the online format, where everyone has equal time and an equal voice, is also rare if not impossible in face-to-face classes. In addition, face-to-face classes are generally favorable to extroverts (Cain, 2012). The online environment makes equal space for those who need time to think, who are more introverted, or whose first language is not English.

The structure of both the course, and of each module, is the reflective process. The course starts with "experience" and moves very slowly through "description" over the course of five modules, to analysis/interpretation, and intelligent action. Each module (there are six, each 2 weeks long, with a seventh concluding module for final projects) is also a container for reflection and a set pattern of activities:

1. An experience
2. Description of the experience
3. Readings
4. Analysis and interpretation of the readings as they relate to the experience and to one's teaching
5. Further analysis in the form of my response to students' posts and the readings
6. Students' responses to my post
7. Feedback on the module

My response to the students' posts and the readings (number 5, above) is perhaps unusual in that it incorporates what students have said in their posts[3] into a lecture on the module content. I bring out what I feel is important about the readings, but use their words and stories to underscore and bring to life what the readings have said, and to respond to important issues that students raise (or miss). From the feedback I have received, I know that students appreciate seeing their own words quoted, my synthesizing responses from across their small-group discussions, and the 10,000-foot view of the readings and their firsthand accounts, that my words provide.

The centerpiece of each module is the experiential activity that begins it. The activity grounds and embodies the readings and also offers a forum for a direct personal encounter with the module content. These, in turn, create opportunities for community and learning from one another. Following are descriptions of the six different modules and activities that students engage in, a reading list for each module, some illustrative student posts, and responses from me. Equally important are the readings, selected to align with the activities and to give teachers (my students) reason to think deeply about their practice. As Adam, a math teacher, said of the readings at the end of the course:

> What best supported my learning were the readings. There wasn't a single reading that I felt didn't have a purpose and for that reason I never felt like this course was giving me work for the sake of giving me work. They all felt very connected and any one reading led beautifully into the next with meaningful connecting ideas.

Learning Stories

Once students have introduced themselves in a brief "Meet Your Classmates" forum, we begin Module 1. Based on my belief that good teaching grows out of attention to learning, Module 1 asks: What is learning?

THE ACTIVITY

To begin, I have students tell a story of a time they "really learned something," either in school or out of school. Tellingly, most choose out-of-school stories. My instructions for the activity, which begins the module, follow:

> Think of a time when you drew upon your capacities and stretched them in ways that took you to a new place where you felt more powerful and capable as a result. This can be a learning experience that happened either in or out of school. Your recollection may or may not have a teacher or other learners in it. The most powerful recollections are those that are full of details. Rather than telling a general kind of learning story (e.g., my grandmother taught me to cook or I learned to drive), tell about a particular time when you learned to cook a particular dish or drive a particular car with note taken of the details of the experience: for example, the setting, the utensils, the smells, the colors, the feel of the tools and ingredients in your hands, the emotions evoked, the steps taken. As you write, please describe the following elements:
>
> - What you learned [the It]
> - Yourself and the impact of your own fears, desires, and motivations on your learning [the Thou/learner]
> - Your peers and their impact on your learning [other Thous]
> - Your teacher (if there was one) and their impact on your learning [the I]
> - The environment and its impact on your learning [Context]

The exhortation to include specifics is the first push to ask students to notice, even in memory, the details of experience. I point them toward the elements of the I, Thou, and It/Context (indicated in brackets above), as this will be one of their first readings (Hawkins, 1974/2002). Students seem to love this activity. They spend time carefully crafting their stories and seem eager to read one another's. When it comes time for my response, I weave their words into my discussion of dimensions of learning apparent both in their stories and in the readings. Below is one example of a learning story written by Adrienne and shared with permission of the author.[4]

The Practice Made a Perfect Lesson

I began learning to play the piano when I was 10 years old. I remember my piano teacher well, Ms. Ellis. She taught me to play the piano at a music studio in Little Rock, Center Stage Music. One particular time I felt good about something in all of my lessons was the time I learned the value of practice. I won a piano competition playing Fur Elise by Beethoven after hours and hours of practice. The setting for the competition was the 4-H center, a log-cabin-like atmosphere on a beautiful and spacious campground. The center was your typical community center type building, though the property rested on land that had a massive surrounding woods and lake for canoeing. I practice Fur Elise for hours to be able to win the competition. I was very young: 13 by that time. Yet, I still remember the feeling of playing very gently during the pianissimos and faster and louder at a forte or a tempo. For that song, it was all about the touch of the keys and the pacing of the notes. It is your classic piano lesson song. Though it is very common, it remains special to me that I learned to play it and won a first place talent trophy for playing it.

The impact of this experience on who I became as a learner is that I learned to appreciate the fine-tuned details of any subject. Similar to paying attention to the weight of my fingers on piano keys, I like to slow down and organize new information in a way that helps me understand how the details work together to create a larger idea. My peers impacted my learning because I continued playing instruments in junior high and high school. I switched to playing the cello after becoming a student in an arts magnet school district offering orchestra. Because the programs at the high school had an arts focus, competitive and dedicated students were attracted to the school. Thus, as I grew into playing the cello, I learned from my peers to continue practicing and paying attention to detail. This learning environment of being around other peers into the arts had a great impact on my dedication to music.

In high school, Ms. Ellis (my former piano teacher) started working at the high school as the Orchestra teacher. She also played the violin! I was happy to be reunited with my piano teacher. In this story, Ms. Ellis is a teacher that continued to impact my learning by reinforcing what she had taught me when I began learning to play the piano at 10 years old. She was my orchestra teacher until I graduated from high school. Coincidentally, Ms. Ellis also went to [the] same hairdresser that I did. I learned many unofficial lessons from her in the beauty salon. She always carried herself with great poise and grace, as if she were at the piano bench or violin stand. I believe I also learned the importance of poise as an important part of the practice.

REFLECTION

Stories ranged from Adrienne's piano playing to Dan P.'s preparation for and eventual climb up Denali with his father and uncle, to Dan C.'s transformation from a self-described "hardened Irish nationalist, hateful towards Northern Irish loyalists," to someone who now saw hate as "a temporary antidote for guilt . . . bred from ignorance." Their stories revealed a lot about each of them, but also supplied me with a virtual library of examples from which to illustrate points about learning. Below, I offer an excerpt from my response to students' stories and responses to the readings. My responses are designed to do several things: to link the activity to the readings; to highlight common themes across their posts; to let them in on what other small groups have discussed; to signal what I see as important for them to understand; and to begin to apply language from the field to some of their everyday experiences. This particular excerpt from my longer response, addresses the role of identity in learning. I attempt to speak directly to the students rather than at an academic remove.

Identity

One's identity is always under construction. It is shaped by one's contexts and interactions with others and the world, and whenever we are in the classroom (or an online learning experience) that is happening—hopefully! If it isn't, if the learning is just the accumulation of facts, like Post-its stuck onto the learner, it won't change the learner. And then, what's the point? You want the learner and her world to expand. Each of your stories told of instances where your world had expanded, and you had been changed.

Dan C.'s story was explicitly one of identity; he identified passionately with Irish Nationalists. In retrospect, he noted that "subscribing to Irish nationalism gave me an identity to be proud of at the expense of others." His learning came with having that identity questioned by a professor who represented the other side of that passion. As a potential victim of it, the professor forced Dan to question himself and his beliefs—his very identity. "I romanticized . . . the IRA for years, and looked up to them. I felt torn, because I also respected this professor. How could I defend the actions of my beloved Irish Nationalists when they threatened the life of my professor? How could I challenge his experience when he was there, and I wasn't?" His assumptions about himself and the world were displaced by a new way of seeing, of perceiving himself and the other. If learning and teaching are about extending one's humanness, they are also about both supporting identity construction as well as critically questioning those identities.

Ben told the story of seeing himself differently as a teacher of writing after getting a response from a teaching colleague whose identity as a writer ran deep and long. Where Ben had been a teacher focused on form, he came to see writing as an expression of the self, and the selves of his students . . . something they gave him as much as he gave them.

In truth, almost all of your stories were about your identities—as musicians, as athletes, as sons and daughters, as seamstresses, as builders, as teachers. If you recognize one thing from this class, I hope it is that your students and you are human-beings-in-the-making, and that you are involved in supporting and expanding that humanity.

The point of beginning the course with students' stories of themselves as learners is to awaken them to Dewey's contention that all learning begins with experience, including their own. Learning that endures comes from what they have engaged in, immersed themselves in. It has changed them in some way. Presence demands curiosity about one's learners. If I can get them curious about themselves and one another as learners, it fortifies their capacity for presence. Additionally, presence asks that teachers know their students:

- What can teachers give their students to do that will reveal who they are?
- What makes them curious?
- What makes them laugh?
- What makes them interested in one another?

One of the readings for the first module is an old piece from Timothy Gallwey's *The Inner Game of Tennis*. Curiously, year after year, this reading has a profound impact on my students. In it Gallwey describes two "selves," Self 1 and Self 2, the Teller and the Doer, respectively (Gallwey, 1974). Self 1, he argues, is constantly getting in the way of Self 2, largely by judging Self 2's performance, thus tangling Self 2 up in self-recrimination and disappointment. My students immediately recognize themselves in this construct and through the rest of the course refer not only to how they are learning to discipline their Self 1 but also to how they are applying their insights with their learners. The reading is not "academic," but it presages much of the brain research that has followed and, most important, signals to them that this course will be useful.

THE READINGS

Gallwey, T. (1974). *The inner game of tennis*. New York, NY: Random House. (Chapters 1 & 2)

Gallwey videos: "Tennis: The Inner Game—Origins" or "An Association for Coaching Interview." Retrieved from theinnergame.com/inner-game-videos/

Hawkins, D. (2002). I, thou, and it. In D. Hawkins, *The informed vision: Essays on learning and human nature* (pp. 51–64). New York, NY: Algora Publishing. (Original work published 1974)

Rodgers, C. (2014). *I, thou, it/contexts* [PowerPoint with notes]. Retrieved from www .academia.edu/8057729/FRAMEWORK_FOR_A_COMMON_LANGUAGE _ABOUT_LEARNING_AND_TEACHING_A_PROPOSAL

The Poem

"miss rosie"

when i watch you
wrapped up like garbage
sitting, surrounded by the smell
of too old potato peels
or
when i watch you
in your old man's shoes
with the little toe cut out
sitting, waiting for your mind
like next week's grocery
i say
when i watch you
you wet brown bag of a woman
who used to be the best looking gal in georgia
used to be called the Georgia Rose
i stand up
through your destruction
i stand up

—Lucille Clifton

THE ACTIVITY

In the second module, I extend students' understanding of learning from their own individual, recollected accounts, to a shared learning experience. Again, the point is to begin to perceive how learning is happening and to see the poem without feeling compelled to "teach" it or to answer the question, "What does the poem mean?" In spite of my instructions, there are always those who think their job is to teach and to "get the answer," but usually other students' stories of their experiences with the poem throw light on the limitations of those approaches. In an introduction to the module, I write:

In the poetry activity you will be learners again. This time, instead of recalling a time that you learned, we will all be learners of the same thing—a poem—and all trying to make sense of that poem together (and with other learners outside our class). This simply gives us more data to draw from when it comes to forming a picture of learning.

In this module my students read Lisa Schneier's (2001) chapter entitled "Apprehending Poetry,"[5] which describes teaching this poem to "low level" high school students in South Boston. Her students entertain many of the same questions my students do, and come to many of the same conclusions. The poem is short but managed to engage Schneier's students for over 6 weeks (6 hours total). I instruct my students to complete the activity *before* reading Schneier's chapter so they can have an unmediated encounter with the poem. When they eventually get to the reading, they do so with heightened curiosity.

My instructions for the activity include the following:

Along with at least one other person (these can be your students, or your partner, or your kids, or friends, or whomever), explore the poem. **You will not be teaching the poem.** You are a fellow explorer *with* your partners, even if they happen to be your students. Please follow all the steps outlined below. You should spend at least 30 minutes on this exercise (I say this in case you think you have it all figured out in 5 minutes. I can guarantee there is more to see than can be "covered" in that amount of time!).

I recommend giving the directions (a–d) to your group and reading them aloud together so that everyone is unified in their understanding of the process.

First Step: All Participants, Please Read Through All the Directions Below Before Beginning

a.   Once you have gathered your fellow explorers, start by having one or two people in the group read the poem out loud twice (more if you feel like it). You might try reading it in a different tone of voice, whispering it, or reading it through in one breath. Make sure everyone has a copy of the poem in front of them. You do not want to be the sole possessor of the poem.

b.   Tell one another what you notice about the poem, not about what it means, at least not for a while. You can each comment on what you notice about the content of the poem (for example, that there seems to be a woman and maybe someone watching her), or about the structure/form of the poem (for example, that there are almost no capital letters or that "i stand up" is repeated). Each time someone states what he or she notices or thinks, ask one another: Where do you see that? What in the poem makes you say that?—gathering the evidence that the speaker is working from. Don't just accept the other person's statement, even if it seems obvious to you. If the other readers in your group say something that someone doesn't follow, they should speak up, not just let it go. Ask one another, "Can you say more?" "Where do you see that?" "What in the poem makes you say that?"

c. You also could each try drawing a picture of what you see in the poem to make visible the mental picture you have of it. Chances are good that you and your co-readers will have very different pictures. Drawing also will help you to notice more details about the content of the poem—what is actually there in the words, what your interpretation is, and what you may have made up and is not in the words at all.

d. As you describe the content and form/language of the poem, meaning will begin to creep into your discussion. When it does, continue to ground your interpretation of the poem in the actual words of the poem. In other words, state your evidence by going back to the words of the poem.

e. After you have discussed the poem with your fellow readers, read the chapter by Lisa Schneier, "Apprehending Poetry."

f. In your post, describe your learning process. What did you notice first? Then what? Then what else? Take note of content and form. How did you build on one another's meanings? What did you draw if you drew a picture? How did the drawings in your group differ? What did you not notice? How did your seeing change or evolve? How did your meanings emerge? How are these meanings grounded in the words of the poem? Or not? Finally, what have you learned about reading poems? How does what you have learned apply to more than just reading poetry?

REFLECTION

The effects of this module, along with the readings, group discussions, and my response, are multiple. First, it forces students to spend time with subject matter long enough to let it show itself. It also opens students' eyes to the fact that reading a poem, and getting something out of it, is a task that they are capable of and that doing so with others can be pleasurable. They see more and differently. Some of them see miss rosie as an old woman, some see her as Black, some as homeless. Some see the narrator as a man, some as a woman, others as a former student, or as miss rosie herself. Some see the narrator as compassionate, others as angry, judgmental, or self-satisfied. My role as teacher is not to judge their conclusions, but to ask for the evidence that supports their views. What I hope they get from the module is all of this, plus a dawning sense of their own power as learners and meaning-makers, along with the realization that this same power lives in their students. If they can give their students subject matter that allows them to engage in the same kind of "productive struggle" (Schoenfeld, 2014) they themselves engaged in, and if they can be interested in what their students say and do, I have moved them a step closer to being present.

THE READINGS

Carini, P. F. (2000). Letter to parents and teachers on some ways of looking at and reflecting on children. In M. Himley (Ed.), *From another angle* (pp. 56–64). New York, NY: Teachers College Press.

Duckworth, E. (2006). The having of wonderful ideas. In *The having of wonderful ideas* (3rd ed., pp. 1–14). New York, NY: Teachers College Press.

Freire, P. (2005). Fourth letter: On the indispensable qualities of progressive teachers for their better performance. In *Teachers as cultural workers: Letters to those who dare teach* (pp. 71–84). Boulder, CO: Westview Press.

Rodgers, C. R. (2001). "It's elementary": The central role of subject matter in learning, teaching, and learning to teach [Review of the book *The roots of literacy*, by D. Hawkins]. *American Journal of Education, 109*(4), 472–480.

Schneier, L. (2001). Apprehending poetry. In E. Duckworth (Ed.), *Tell me more* (pp. 42–78). New York, NY: Teachers College Press.

Swartz, T. (1978). On feedback. *Educational Solutions Newsletter*, pp. 5–10. issuu .com/eswi/docs/1109_-4-on-feedback-april-1978

The Leaf Activity

This is one of my favorite modules and if it is taught in the autumn, it's even better. More on why in a minute. In this module I again ask students to slow down and *see*. They are still looking at themselves and their own learning rather than at their students and their learning, but they begin to make those connections in Module 3.

THE ACTIVITY

In this module I have students read a piece by S. H. Scudder entitled "The Student, the Fish, and Agassiz," written in 1879 by a former pupil of Harvard professor Louis Agassiz,[6] famous for his study of fish. Scudder was instructed by Agassiz to observe a dead fish. "'Take this fish,' said he, 'and look at it; we call it a Haemulon [pronounced Hemyú-lon]; by and by I will [return and] ask what you have seen'" (p. 450). After 3 hours, Scudder thinks he has seen all there possibly is to see of the "ghastly" dead fish, but Agassiz is nowhere to be found. Finally, after more hours and out of desperation, Scudder decides he will draw the fish. When Agassiz finally returns he is happy to see that Scudder has chosen this strategy. "The pencil is one of the best eyes," he says. But he is not satisfied with what Scudder has seen. "Look again," he exhorts Scudder, "Look again!" This went on for "three long days," Scudder writes, each day revealing how much he had missed the day before (p. 453).

I wanted to create a similar experience for my students, minus the dead fish. Enter the leaves. In the fall, in the northern United States, and especially in the northeast, the leaves (maple leaves in particular) turn dazzling shades of red, copper, yellow, brown, and gold, and sometimes all of these at once. For the activity, I ask students go outside, gather a small pile of leaves of the same type, and bring them inside. They are then to choose one, putting the other leaves aside for the moment. In a medium (or media) of their choice—pencil, colored pencil, pen, paint brush, crayon, watercolor, oil paints; on paper, canvas, rock, or the computer—it doesn't matter—they are to spend at least 30 minutes drawing their leaf. Once they have finished, they are to put their leaf back in the pile of leaves, mix them up, and see whether they can find their leaf.

Once they have finished, they are to post their drawing, which I then put into a Leaf Album (a PowerPoint slide show) for all to share. Some of their drawings are stunning, others rudimentary, but they all convey something of the artist.

REFLECTION

When the album is finally assembled, I find it quite moving. As with the poem, many begin with fear and self-judgment: "I am not an artist!" As one student wrote, "At first the leaf activity was my worst nightmare." The quality of their drawings is, of course, less important than the quality of their experience, which, usually, is one of wonder and delight. It is not an exaggeration to say that some students fall in love with their leaves. Many decide to keep their leaf around. Some name them—Hannah and Larry are two names that come to mind. As Gregory wrote, "Strangely enough, I am having a hard time parting ways with my leaf. It is still sitting on my coffee table in my living room."

The time spent contemplating this activity brings delight but can raise profound issues, too: the inevitability of decay, impermanence, affection and loss, the "experience" of the leaf itself and its life cycle, and even, as Stefani wrote, the power of naming. In her response to a post by Nicholas (whose 3-year-old daughter named Nicholas's leaf Larry), she wrote: "You mentioned that your daughter named the leaf. I was particularly struck by this parenthetical comment, and think it's much more important than its place in your description. There is something very powerful about naming things, and people. We think differently about our students when we think of them by name. With names comes individuality." Nicholas responded that by spending time attending so carefully to something, "you definitely do feel like the it (the leaf, in this case) is a friend of sorts, and one you feel like you want to get to know better and better." I am reminded of a quote by biologist Barbara McClintock (as quoted in Keller, 1983): "I know every plant in the field. I know them intimately, and find it a great pleasure to know them" (p. 198).

The students all comment on how much they noticed about leaves that they'd never taken note of before: tiny holes, dark spots, variegated colors (the whole realm of color comes into play—how do you replicate that kind of green-gold or copper?), veins (which resemble the structure of a tree—a fractal), the convex shape of the tip of the stem (why?), and so forth. "I've seen leaves my whole life, but I've never really *seen* a leaf," they comment. "I'll never look at a tree the same way again."

The potential depth and complexity of this exercise are further brought forth by Stefani in her response. She ponders what it means to see, and one's responsibility to the object of her observation. As she suggests, while students are certainly more complex than leaves, the exercise raises questions about the seriousness of "seeing" and drawing conclusions about human beings.

> As I undertook the leaf exercise, I was struck by the difference between a good "eye" and a good "voice." In other words, my experience of the leaf activity was that the task of drawing the leaf helped me to look at it more closely, yet at the same time I found myself struggling with how poorly my drawing conveyed what I was seeing. I saw its size, so close to the size of my own hand; the intricacy of the vein structure; the mold spots; the shininess of one side that contrasted with the velvety softness of the other; the tear in one end; the irregular place that interrupted the smooth line of one edge; the almost infinite variations in the colors—which, I note now have changed since I looked at it yesterday, lightening along one edge as the leaf dries out further—and many other details. I despaired, however, at getting all of those details into my drawing. My drawing looks like a leaf, to be sure. It might even look like a Magnolia leaf. But it doesn't really look like *my* leaf (which I was able to re-find fairly easily among the handful I brought indoors). The colors are not nearly saturated enough, the shininess doesn't come across at all, and my little hatchings don't even come close to capturing the fascinating variety of shapes of the veins. Some of my frustration was with the medium: I found myself thinking longingly about oil paints and "dirty pour" canvases as I looked at the way the spots of green, black, white, and tan swirled into each other on the leaf, forming amoeba-shaped bull's-eyes and other interesting patterns. Colored pencil—at least in my inexperienced hands—just wasn't fluid enough to duplicate what I was seeing. Some of my frustration was with my perceived clumsiness with the pencils: there seemed to be a disconnect between my brain and my hand as I struggled to duplicate the shapes I was seeing, desperately trying to recapture the feeling of competence I used to have in long-ago art classes. Some of my frustration was with the knowledge that if I had given myself a week to do this drawing, instead of a couple of hours, it might look entirely different. There seemed to be another frustration, though, that was more essential—an idea of doing justice to the leaf by depicting it properly, giving it voice—that seems to tie in with the idea of "morality" that was raised in the instructions to this post.

If an encounter with a leaf can raise these complex questions, imagine the implications when the "leaf" is another human being. Gregory (a high school social studies teacher) took a different tack. He looked through the lens of his own teaching practice and ruminated on Agassiz's willingness to push Scudder to keep at the task through his frustration. Here he reflects on his own students and his expectations of them:

What if I forced my students to keep going—regardless of whether they felt like they could not go anymore. I think I may try this activity with my students and a small passage of text. I will ask them to close-read the passage instead of being satisfied after they brainstorm some thought. I will ask for more and more. Ask them to draw the passage, act the passage, explain the passage and anything else that I can think of.

The simplicity of the exercise, along with its personal impact, allows students to see connections to their own practice and to raise their own questions, which, if I had raised them, would be less powerful. They would be *my* questions rather than theirs.

Having completed the leaf exercise, a relatively feel-good activity with some beautiful results[7] (especially in the fall), students have begun to feel the benefits of slowing down in order to see what there is to see. They also have begun to sense the complexity and richness of what is before them, even in something as simple as a leaf or an 18-line poem. What else might they perceive in life if they were present to it? In my response, I often comment on the place of beauty in learning—how it is revealed if one takes the time, both with the subject matter and with one's students. Dan C. wrote in response, "We all have stories of students who endure struggles that can be overlooked or misinterpreted. I understand that there are times we must take action. However, there is a peculiar beauty about our students. Simply being aware of this will make a difference in how we as educators form our I–Thou bond." With their curiosity awakened, it is time to complicate things a bit. And so we move to Module 4: The Gun and the Naked Woman.

THE READINGS

Rodgers, C. (2002). Defining reflection: Another look at John Dewey and reflective thinking. *Teachers College Record, 74*(4), 842–866.

Scudder, S. H. (1879). The student, the fish, and Agassiz: By the student. In *American poems* (3rd ed.; pp. 450–454). Boston, MA: Houghton, Osgood & Co. Retrieved from www.skidmore.edu/~mmarx/L&EF09/agassiz.pdf

The Gun and the Naked Woman

The goal of this module is to bring my students' attention to the filters through which they attend to and make meaning of what they see—from students' work to students themselves. What are the assumptions that shape what they see? Where do these assumptions come from? Do they hold water? Can they be trusted? Another skill I want students to develop is the ability to discern the difference between an observation, an interpretation, and a judgment. Finally, I want them to become alert to the contextual forces that shape their meaning-making.

THE ACTIVITY

Having shared stories of learning, spent time with a poem, and contemplated the complexities of a leaf, I now ask them to describe a 16-year-old boy's pencil sketch of a gun, seemingly recently fired by the hand holding it, and a naked woman. The gun has tendrils of smoke rising from its barrel. Below and to the right is a second sketch, much simpler in its lines, of a naked woman, sitting on what appears to be a street corner, leaning against a brick wall, her legs drawn up under her, and with what looks like a tear coming down one cheek. Her right hand is up to her face and her left arm holds the weight of her body. The artist has rendered the hand and gun in carefully drawn detail with attention to shading, proportion, and dimensionality. The woman on the other hand seems drawn as an afterthought. There are few details and the drawing feels flat in comparison. The drawing originally was done on 8.5" x 11" paper. (See Figure V.1.)

As a large group, students are instructed to describe what they see over the course of 3 days. Each time, they are to try to add something new that had not yet been mentioned by others. On the third day, they reflect on the experience. For the most part, students stay descriptive, but I suspect that beneath the discipline of their comments there are unvoiced worries and perhaps judgments about the artist. When I reveal, at the end of day 3, that the artist was my son, and share his statement about his motivations, my students reveal these worries and their surprise at learning who the artist was. Here is the artist's statement, written when he was 21:

Figure V.1. Drawing by a 16-Year-Old Boy

Jon: The assignment was to draw an inanimate object in great detail,
without referencing the object, and to put it in a human context
(meaning that the object had to be used by a human, or at least
present in a human setting). The teacher gave us examples like
people drinking tea, and we could draw the tea set in great detail,
or, as another example, draw a musical instrument.

    I drew the gun in hand for a couple reasons: (1) to push the
envelope. I didn't want to draw a dumb tea set or a clarinet;
I wanted to draw something cool. (2) I was a sophomore in
high school: therefore guns = cool. (3) The smoking gun was a
romanticized image for me, mostly because of movies, and I added
the rest of the drawing as a space filler, to balance the drawing
visually. I chose the naked woman and the brick wall/back alley
setting because I wanted to give the drawing some grit, and I knew
that would grab the attention of the viewer, regardless of whether
it made them curious, angry, disturbed, whatever. It made them
SOMETHING. That was all I was really considering when I chose
to draw the rest besides the gun.

(CR to Jon: What feelings, if any, did you have about the subjects you
chose?)

Jon: They were all forbidden things. I'd never used or even held a gun;
maybe I'd never even seen a real one. I'd never been with a woman,

and cities and back alleys were still a foreign concept to me, having grown up in rural Vermont. I was using the art to explore, and to provoke, but not as a release.

REFLECTION

The drawing was done in 2002. The Columbine shootings in Colorado had happened in 1999, and the unending series of tragic school shootings we have seen since had not yet happened. In addition, there was no cable TV where we were, and my children watched little TV. Living in rural Vermont at the time, access to the Internet was still nonexistent for us. Video games were forbidden in our home, and Jon's exposure to media violence was minimal. However, the lenses that my students bring to their interpretation of these drawings stand in contrast to Jon's experience and are a product of their time. One student, Pete, an elementary school physical education teacher, wrote:

> After reading everyone's posts and reflecting on the drawing multiple times, I found myself frequently typing then deleting. This was because I kept making assumptions based on what I saw, instead of seeing just details (lines, rectangles, other shapes, etc.). . . . [The artist] being a 16-year-old boy, it automatically came into my mind the fear of school violence and school shootings.

Another student, Samantha, an elementary school special education teacher, became acutely aware of her own emotional response to the drawing and the value of not running with first impressions:

> One thing I found really interesting about my perspective as a teacher is my emotional connection with this picture. . . . I think if . . . one of my students drew this picture, it would be quite alarming to me, as it focuses on both guns (violence) and women. It also alarmed me that we can continuously make prejudgments [of] students' expressions. I immediately took this as a gun-related violation or gun control art, while it may have been a cry for help or a way that this 16-year-old boy was expressing himself based on the past, or other video games that he has seen or have [sic] been exposed to. I think it's really important to look at the beauty in things, and not be so judgmental at our first impressions of pictures or student work.

I appreciate Samantha's point that "the beauty in things" also can be evident in art that is disturbing. There is skill in the drawing, an aesthetic that can be obscured by its content. The point is not to ignore drawings like this one and what they *might* mean, but to make sure one has sufficient evidence for the conclusions one is drawing (think back to the poem). The point is also to be present to what *is* there, and not to what one *imagines* is there. And finally, the point is to know oneself, one's assumptions, and the various sociocultural and personal lenses through which one is making meaning, especially of others. As Pete said in his reflection:

> After finding out that it was our Professor's son's drawing, who is seemingly innocent and kind, I almost felt bad[8] for making judgments too soon that were clearly untrue. Not only could I relate as a teacher, but I have learned to take a much more in-depth look at my students before figuring that they just act the way they do because it is who they are.

And Stefani:

> Remembering the importance of taking time for description before moving on to judgment, and of insisting on clarification before decisions are made, is critical. I would go so far as to say that there is moral significance to careful description, to taking the time to see things for what they actually are, and that the readings and activities of this module support that stance.

To be present includes the self-discipline to withhold judgment, to, as Dewey (1933) says, "endure suspense and . . . undergo the trouble of searching" the evidence (p. 124). It is, indeed, a moral stance, as is the commitment to presence itself. Being present, in other words, is not a matter of fluff or "feel good" teaching; it is work, and work on the self as much as on one's practice.

THE READINGS

Carini, P. (2002). Meditation on description. In P. Carini, *Starting strong* (pp. 163–164). New York, NY: Teachers College Press.

Seidel, S. (1998). Learning from looking. In N. Lyons (Eds.), *With portfolio in hand: Validating the new teacher professionalism* (pp. 69–89). New York, NY: Teachers College Press.

Weingarten, G. (2007, April 8). Pearls before breakfast. *The Washington Post.* Retrieved from www.washingtonpost.com/wp-dyn/content/article/2007/04/04/AR2007040401721.html

Descriptive Feedback

In the fifth module I ask my students to bring their own students into the process of reflection and description. They are to ask their students for descriptive feedback,[9] which I define as feedback given *by students to teachers* on their experiences as learners in a dedicated, dialogic, reflective third space. This turns the commonly held notion of feedback, where teachers tell students how they're doing, on its head. Here, students tell teachers how they—the students—are doing, what is helping their learning, what is getting in the way, and what they would like to do next. It implicates the teacher and his or her teaching, but is a step shy of evaluating it, which is not the job of the student. The purpose of the module is to bring my students to an appreciation of their students as valuable, and usually untapped, resources who can contribute to their shared project of teaching and learning. Additionally, and again, I mean to cultivate an awareness that what they see is not always what they think they see. Using descriptive feedback opens up the notion that reflection is not only about one's teaching and how well or badly it has gone, but about students and their learning, about all there is to be present to, and how one needs to respond.

THE ACTIVITY

The activity that grounds this module is to carry out a 20-minute lesson with learners followed by 10 minutes of learner feedback on their learning. My students are given a list of feedback questions to ask (see Figure V.2) and they are admonished to adhere to those questions. The questions are designed to keep the attention on the students and their learning rather than on the teachers themselves and their teaching. (I have had teachers ignore the questions and jump directly to questions like, "So, how'd I do?" which, obviously, misses the point.) Teachers are encouraged to ask follow-up, probing questions like, "Can you say more?" or "Can you give me an example?" They also are asked to respond to students' offerings with "understanding responses"[10] ("What I think you are saying is . . . Is that right?"), which verify that (or whether) they have understood the student correctly. These efforts usually spur further clarification by the student and more information for the teacher. One of my students once

Figure V.2. Suggested Feedback Questions

- "What did you learn? What will you still know/be able to do tomorrow?" (This is a different question from "What did I teach?" or "What did we do?" It really asks learners to consider to what extent they have internalized what was taught.)
- "How do you know you learned it?" (This helps students avoid telling you what they were "supposed" to learn as opposed to what they really learned.)
- "What helped your learning?"
- "What got in the way of your learning? What was confusing?"
- "What would have helped your learning more?"
- (If there was something that happened during the lesson that puzzled you [the teacher], where you weren't sure you were following the learning, you can ask students about it. You might say, "When you were doing [whatever it was], what was going on? I saw you doing x, but I wasn't sure what you were thinking. What were you thinking?" as a way of understanding better what happened. This question is obviously optional and dependent upon whether something happened during the lesson that piqued your curiosity.)
- "How did you feel during the lesson?"
- "Is there anything else you want me to know?"

---

likened the process to raising the hood of a car to find out what is going on in the engine. Just because the car moves doesn't necessarily mean that all is well.

REFLECTION

Adam (a high school math teacher) described his experience this way:

> Descriptive feedback is an instructional concept that most teachers believe they do. However, through the materials in this module it is clearly evident that [for] most teachers . . . their process . . . is truly flawed. After completing the readings and the teaching activity I can openly admit that I am one of those teachers. The flaw in my process was not my intentions but [was] clearly in the questions I would ask. I say this because it has become clear to me that I was always focusing more on the subject and content of what was being taught rather than *how the students learned it.* I was clearly getting too caught up in what I was teaching rather than how my students were learning, and without meaning to had convinced myself that the key to their success was changing the material to meet their needs, rather than having their learning abilities, weaknesses, and styles mold how I used the material (emphasis added).

The feedback dialogue is grounded in the teacher's curiosity about the learners' experience and a genuine desire to serve the learners in the best ways possible. It is not a process of giving power over to students but one of creating both room for their powers to thrive and a space for a teacher–student partnership. Power is not a zero-sum game where giving students power or authority means giving up one's own. Echoing Adam, Freire (2005), in his chapter on listening to learners (see readings below), makes a distinction between democratic and authoritarian teachers, emphasizing the role of power. Authoritarian teachers, he writes, "are preoccupied with evaluating the students, with seeing whether they are following or not." However, he writes, if teachers

> choose to be democratic, . . . then in their scholarly daily lives, which they live constantly subject to critical analysis, they live the difficult but possible and pleasurable experience of speaking to and with learners. They know that dialogue centered not only on the content to be taught but on life itself, if it is true, not only is valid from the point of view of the act of teaching, but also prepares an open and free climate in the ambience of their classroom. (p. 115)

The simplest indication I see of this democratic disposition in a teacher is this: when a teacher asks a student a question to which he does not already have an answer. He listens, in other words, for *the student's* answer rather than for *his*. It is part of the process of humanizing the classroom, creating a space that grants learners, and especially children, the authority to voice their experiences and recognize their own power to contribute to decisions that most directly affect them. Again, it is imperative that teachers also be present to their own motives so they can hear and see their students clearly. Being present does not mean going into the dialogue free of one's own motives. It means bringing awareness to them.

Descriptive feedback is a training tool for presence. It disciplines the teacher to listen, to *not* know, to be curious, to inquire, and to grow. It is vital that presence, and teaching itself, be seen as a process of inquiry (reflection) and experimentation, and not merely as an individual endeavor, but as shared. I tell students that it would be folly in any relationship to never check in with the other to see how that relationship is working: "What's going on for you? How is this working for you? For us? What do you need? What do I need from you?" It assumes, as Freire says, love for and solidarity with students. A large part of the feedback dialogue is to provide learners with language for their experience—"naming the world"—a phrase to which I've referred many times. It's that important!

A final caveat: One of the tricky tasks for the teacher is to give students—especially young children—the language for their experience without putting words in their mouths. That is, children often do not have the vocabulary to express what they are thinking and feeling. As the teacher searches for words that might match those feelings and thoughts, she also has to teach what those words mean. The challenge is to convey the meaning of the words to the child without displacing the child's thoughts and feelings. Constant checking for understanding and providing rich and redundant explanations (through synonyms, gestures, stories, pictures) are imperative.

THE READINGS

Freire, P. (2005). Seventh letter: From talking to learners to talking to them and with them; from listening to learners to being heard by them. In *Teachers as cultural workers: Letters to those who dare teach* (pp. 111–121). Boulder, CO: Westview Press.

Rodgers, C. (2006). Attending to student voice: The impact of descriptive feedback on learning and teaching. *Curriculum Inquiry, 36*(2), 209–227.

Rodgers, C. (2018). Descriptive Feedback: Students voice in K-5 classrooms. *The Australian Educational Researcher*, 45(1), 87–102. doi.org/10.1007/s13384 -018-0263-1.

Descriptive Review of a Learner

Starting in Module 1 and throughout the course, students are required to describe and document, from five different angles, a learner of their choice, as outlined in Himley's volume, *From Another Angle* (2000).[11] At the end of the course, they write up the final "Descriptive Review" bookended by their rationale for choosing the learner and a reflection on the process. The purpose of the Descriptive Review is to take the time to really see one child: one that slips through the cracks, is annoying, or is a "highflyer" who gets left alone because they are no trouble. As one student, Nicholas, wrote, "The whole course perfectly built up to this module."

THE ACTIVITY

Here are the initial instructions that students are given in Module 1:

> One of the major tasks for the course will be to write a Descriptive Review of a learner. This can be a child in one of your classes, one of your own children, the child of a friend, or a sibling or other relative. There is no age limit, although I would caution against describing a spouse, a parent, a partner, or a coworker. You will be working on this description throughout the course, but you will not post your full description until near the end of the course. You will be observing and gathering "evidence" for your description starting in the next module, and posting your observation notes in your (online) journal. I will check these and give you feedback when needed. To get an overview of the process, please read the chapter entitled "A Letter to Teachers and Parents" by Patricia Carini (Himley, 2000) in which she identifies five angles from which to observe: (1) physical appearance and gesture; (2) strong interests and preferences; (3) connections with others; (4) disposition and temperament; and (5) modes of thinking and learning. You must provide details about each angle.
>
> Over the course of Module 1 please identify a learner whom you would like to observe. I would suggest someone who seems to slip through the cracks, whom you would like to know better, or who intrigues you. If you choose to describe a child, I would recommend

contacting the parents, explaining the assignment to them, sharing the "Letter to Parents and Teachers" (see Readings), and asking their permission, saying you would be happy to share the review with them once you've finished. (If there are other procedures that your school follows, please attend to those as well. If you need an explanatory statement from me, I can provide that.) In some cases, parents also have become involved in the observations and can offer valuable insights. In the past, many of my students also have let their learners know that this is a project they have for graduate school, and that they would like the learners' help in completing it. Learners are usually very excited to participate in their teacher's "homework."

Sometimes students feel uneasy about this assignment, as though they are being asked to "spy" on their learners. What Carini makes clear is that we are *always* observing our students, but we seldom take the time to see whether what we think we see is what is really there. We see so many learners in a day, especially at the secondary level, and it is easy to jump to conclusions about who they are (even our own children!) without ever really taking the time to *just see* them. And students will tell you it isn't often that they *feel* truly seen by their teachers.

REFLECTION

In Module 1 students think about a learner and, without observing them yet, try to fill out the five categories from memory. This often serves to highlight for teachers how little they actually know about their learner and also to pique their curiosity to find out more. In subsequent modules I instruct students to observe from one angle, moving systematically through all five, and revising previous entries as they gather more observations. I encourage students to write using as much detail as possible, as they did with their learning stories, being specific and telling about a "time when." This provides vivid accounts of the particulars of a child in action.[12] Here is a good example of a "time when," written by Pete, an elementary-level physical education teacher. His kids were engaged in a group "turn style" jump rope activity, and his chosen learner is "T":

With T, his thinking and learning both seem to come [through] most strongly when he is confident with the particular topic and when he seems to be having a good day prior to class. During the problem-solving unit, he used his intelligence to come up with solutions for two activities. I will use [one] activity to explain his thought process here.
. . . After there was a lack of communication between numerous pairs, I again asked the class if anyone had other ideas. T raised his hand once more and suggested that in order to maintain rhythm,

students would go right after the rope passed by the person in front
of them, one after the other after the other, etc. This idea is really the
solution to how to succeed in the activity, as decided by myself and the
other P.E. teacher at school. I could tell by T's interest in the activity,
he had been brainstorming and thinking hard [about] how his class
could successfully break the record.

The particulars of this description bring T's problem-solving capacities
and enthusiasm alive in a much more vivid way than "T is a good problem-
solver" would have. In addition, before observing T, Pete was unaware of
what a great problem-solver T was, only that he was a handful.

   While my direct input into the writing of their reviews is minimal, I
do provide several examples of exemplary reviews. In addition, students
are given a rubric (see Appendix) by which to assess one other person's review. This is meant as a formative assessment aimed at mutual support and
friendly critique. I think this has been successful in some cases, and not in
others, leading me to consider groups of three rather than pairs. The tension
is always one of time. Reading and commenting on two reviews will take
more time (and all my students are incredibly pressed for time), but also will
provide more feedback.

   In the end, the exercises in learning to see explored in Modules 1
through 5, along with the ongoing regular assignment to gather evidence for
their Descriptive Reviews, has prepared them fairly well for the final project.
They have come to appreciate the benefits of slowing down to see and the
difference between observation and judgment. As Carini (2001) writes, "To
describe is to value" (p. 164). I have found that in the very act of observing
and subsequent documentation, teachers' perceptions of the learner change.
Pete explains his own learning below:

   Throughout the last few weeks, this process has allowed me to gain
   a wealth of knowledge with regard to my particular student. Due
   to my prior experiences with T, I had very few positive things to say
   about him. Most of the time while watching the class as a whole, the
   attention I was giving him was in the form of discipline, reacting to
   his behavior. After viewing him more closely and digging deeper into
   his learning, it is now clear to me that there is another side to this
   child. A side that celebrates successes, attempts to make relationships
   with everyone, and most importantly, wants to learn and be great.
   There were so many instances where I could see through what he was
   showing on the outside. Over time it was apparent that a positive
   end result for lessons of basketball, project adventure, and circus arts
   was his driving factor and he would usually show this through rare
   yet unforgettable emotions of happiness and excitement. I could not
   have even imagined that this would be the result of more articulate
   observation of my learner, but I am certainly glad it was.

As a student, teacher, and adult in general, my experience throughout this time definitely allowed me to learn substantially. The importance of in-depth observation has never been clearer to me when it comes to truly understanding our learners. . . . I often found myself spending too much time watching only some of my students, and, therefore, leaving the others to almost just exist in the environment. To one day be the teacher that I have set out to be, I now understand the importance of diving deeper into not only my students and their learning, but also their "forces of context."

Adam's experience was similar, even though he dealt with a "normal" student who previously had given him no trouble:

The most significant learning I had in the course definitely came with the conclusion of my descriptive review of a learner. I didn't expect to get much from the study of my learner since I was focusing on a student characterized as "normal," but I wound up learning far more than I initially anticipated. She showed me just how complex even a typical student's learning process can be, and due to this I need to be far more aware of the differentiating factors that exist in every student's learning.

My students will sometimes complain that they can't possibly do a descriptive review of all their students. Fair enough. But I respond with something I call my "grain of sand theory." It goes like this: It is admittedly unfeasible to closely examine every grain of sand on a beach. However, if you take the time to look closely at just one or two grains of sand, you can learn a whole lot about the nature of a beach, without having to look at millions of grains. As Adam says, he is now aware that multiple factors exist in every student's learning.

When students learn how much there is to see, they generally want to see more. As Nicholas said after the leaf activity, "You definitely do feel like the it (the leaf, in this case) is a friend of sorts, and one you feel like you want to get to know better and better." Observation and description ignite both curiosity and affection, both essential to presence. Dewey (1916) writes, "Attention means caring for a thing, in the sense of both affection and of looking out for its welfare" (p. 192). He also points out that engagement with the world implies our inseparability from it. He notes that our own well-being, including the well-being of our planet, is entwined with those whom we teach. Our presence to them benefits not only the students, but the teacher as well. One can see from entries like Pete's and Adam's that they are personally invested in the task and see that the benefits accrue not just to their chosen students but to all their students, and to themselves. As Dewey said, we are with one another in a developing situation. In other words, we're all in it together.

THE READINGS

Abu-El Haj, T. R. (2003). Equity from the standpoint of the particular. *Teachers College Record, 105*(5), 817–845.

Carini, P. (2010). The power of the particular. In P. F. Carini & M. Himley, *Jenny's story* (pp. 58–63). New York, NY: Teachers College Press.

Carini, P. F., & Himley, M. (2010). Descriptive review of the child. In P. F. Carini & M. Himley, *Jenny's story* (pp. 23–34). New York, NY: Teachers College Press.

Rodgers, C. R. (2010). The role of descriptive inquiry in building presence and civic capacity. In N. Lyons (Ed.), *Handbook of reflective inquiry* (pp. 45–61). New York, NY: Springer.

CHAPTER 13

Conclusion

What I have described here is just one course. While I can confidently say, based on student feedback, that the course makes a difference in my students' lives and practice, I am not ignorant of the forces of context that face them, especially those who teach in U.S. public schools. For the most part, they do not work in caring systems. Perhaps systems, by definition, don't care. But what if they did? What if systems, which, while monolithic from one perspective, also are made up of individual human beings, sought to humanize rather than measure? To be responsible *to* teachers and children, rather than overseers of accountability? The former seeks to bring forth the best, the latter to ferret out the weaknesses.

"ARE YOU OKAY?"

I have learned over the years of teaching this course online that being responsible to my students—present to them and all the complex demands of their lives—*results* in their being accountable. My students are adults, most in their 20s and early 30s. They are, for the most part, new teachers. Because they are starting out in life, many are in new jobs, and some start new jobs in the middle of the course, sometimes moving from one home to another. They are paying off college loans and simultaneously assuming debt for graduate school. (The state of New York mandates that all teachers have their master's degree within 5 years of initial certification.) Many of them are in relationships that turn to marriage or break up in the course of my class. Many are coaches who not only teach all day, but coach all afternoon. Some are taking more than one online class. In the 3 months we are together, some are pregnant, some give birth, some lose grandparents or even parents. I can pretty much count on birth and death happening, and say as much from the get-go. Others work in demanding urban or rural contexts with even more complications. "Chances are that things will happen to scramble your plans," I say. I beg them to "just keep me in the loop, so we can figure out what to do together."

Inevitably, especially in the online environment, students fall behind. I have found that their default reaction to this situation is shame. They are embarrassed and ashamed that they have not kept up, and this keeps them from contacting me, despite my explicit pleas. While I may have had an initial twinge of resentment for their having disappeared, for not being "accountable," I have learned to curb that initial reaction. Instead, I have come to see the power of a simple three-word question: "Are you okay?" Almost always, when I ask, I find that, no, in fact, they are *not* okay. Life happens, and it is happening to them. They generally are doing their best and are so hard on themselves that I don't need to be. The power of this question is somewhat amazing to me. It is an expression of concern rather than a judgment (as, for example, reinforcing the course absence policy might be), which seems to invite gratitude rather than defensiveness. And this seems to open the door to finding a way, together, to make it possible to get the work done.

This semester, I had a student, I'll call him Sam, whose life pretty much fell apart. He disappeared and after several emails from me I still had not heard from him. His posts up until he disappeared had been strong and he didn't strike me as the type to blow off the course. Where I might normally feel irritated, I held out the possibility that everything might not be okay. Finally, I did hear. It turned out that Sam's wife, who was due to give birth in 2 months, had experienced complications. Suddenly, their daughter was born 2 months premature, with health problems. In addition, his wife's health problems persisted. In the meantime, Sam's colleague at his urban charter school had to leave and he had to take on her responsibilities on top of his own. These problems persisted throughout the course. Many, many times I needed to check in with Sam to ask if he was okay. In the end, although not always exactly on time, Sam finished the course and finished it beautifully. In his final feedback to me he wrote:

> I have not explicitly acknowledged it, but the faith that you demonstrated in my devotion to invest in the lessons despite my personal complications has brought out the best in me in the last three modules. Rather than take your generous accommodations and abuse them by doing the bare minimum, I found myself spending a great deal of time on each post, in some ways wanting to "make up" with quality what I clearly have been lacking in timeliness. This is something I need to examine more in myself personally and also how I could leverage this with students—finding ways to further empower the strengths that already exist while addressing the shortcomings.

FINAL THOUGHTS

I am one person and this is the story of just one course. I teach in a large state university system and I cannot say its policies are moving toward presence. We are asked almost daily to do more with less and do it better with more students. The corporatization of the university is as rampant as the corporatization of healthcare. Even the language is changing—marketing trends, efficiency, return on investment. I keep thinking that the other shoe will drop and schools and universities will realize that the kinds of minds and souls these policies produce are so much poorer than they might be with more humanizing policies. But so far we seem hell-bent on business models being the answer. To what? How to be number one?

Nonetheless I remain hopeful, in large part because of students like Sam, Ben, Maureen, Pete, Stefani, Sarah, Nicholas, Samantha, Gregory, Adrienne, Adam, Dan P., and Dan C. I know they care about being present. When new teachers come to me in despair for what is happening in schools, I tell them that I am sustained by something attributed to Mahatma Gandhi, words to the effect that "whatever you do will be insignificant, but it is very important that you do it." The dailiness of teaching can feel insignificant, but it is not insignificant for children, for their families, for their communities, for our democracy, for the planet. Far from it. It is vital. For every teacher to whom I am present, there will be a teacher who feels seen, and for every teacher who feels seen, there will be a child who also will feel seen. And so presence gets paid forward. This is my firm belief. This is my fervent hope.

I leave you with Sarah's words:

> This course has changed the way I think about myself, my teaching, my learning, my students, and my students' learning. Additionally, this course has changed the way I plan to teach in my future classroom. This course changed the way I view online classes, and graduate school. I now feel ready and excited to continue learning and [to] strive to be the best teacher I can be.

Appendix: Rubric for Descriptive Reviews

Criteria	Physical appearance and gesture	Strong interests and preferences	Connections with others	Disposition and temperament	Modes of thinking and learning
USE OF THE PARTICULAR					
(Superior) Each description of the person is backed up with evidence. The evidence comes in the form of a story about a time when this was observed or related to the writer. The story is filled with particular details that bring the child and the scene to life.					
(Average) Most of the descriptions of the person are backed up with evidence. The evidence sometimes comes in the form of a story about a time when this was observed or related to the writer. There are some descriptions that are not supported by evidence. The story has a moderate level of detail and it is possible to form a picture of the child, although some parts are unclear.					
(Unacceptable) Few of the descriptions of the person are backed up with evidence. There are only a few stories about the person, and it is difficult to form a clear picture of them.					
RESPECT FOR THE PERSON (AND THE FAMILY)					
(Superior) The description shows a high degree of regard for the learner. There is little judgmental language and a strong general orientation toward the learner's strengths.					

(Average) The description shows a moderate degree of regard for the learner. There is some judgmental language and some tendency to focus on the weaknesses, lacks, or failings of the learner.			
(Unacceptable) The description shows a low regard for the learner. There is a considerable amount of judgmental language and a strong tendency to focus on the weaknesses, lacks, or failings of the learner.			

QUALITY OF THE WRITING

(Superior) Free of spelling and grammar errors, lively, vivid language, engaging narrative.			
(Average) A moderate number of spelling and grammar errors, some lively and vivid passages, mostly engaging narrative.			
(Unacceptable) Lots of spelling and grammar errors, confusing or lackluster use of language. Hard to get through.			

General comments:

1. How did the description leave you feeling?
2. What particular strengths did you see in both the child and the review itself?

Notes

Part I

1. I use the masculine and feminine pronouns to distinguish between learner and teacher when they appear in the same sentence. Since, according to 2016 UNESCO figures, most teachers in the world are women (53% in secondary school and 65% in primary school), I have chosen to refer to the teacher as a "she."

2. I focus here on only one tradition, Insight Meditation, or Vipassana from the Theravada tradition, which originates primarily from Sri Lanka, Burma, Thailand, Laos, and Cambodia. It was introduced in the United States in the 1970s by Joseph Goldstein, Sharon Salzberg, and Jack Kornfield, each of whom has gone on to write numerous books on the subject. Together they established the Insight Meditation Society (IMS) in 1975 and two retreat sites in Massachusetts and California. In 1979, Jon Kabat-Zinn, another well-known teacher, physician, and author, established Mindfulness-Based Stress Reduction (MBSR) and initiated a now long-established field of brain research on the effects of mindfulness practice on physical and mental states.

3. I am deeply indebted to my colleagues Claire Stanley and Jack Millet, co-founders of Vermont Insight Meditation Center in Brattleboro. Whatever accuracies occur here are thanks to them. All errors and limitations in understanding are mine alone.

4. I need to make a distinction between presence in teaching and what is referred to in the online world as a "teaching presence," whose focus has more to do with facilitation and management of online courses.

Part II

1. Dewey first mentions the attitude of directness in *Democracy and Education* (1916), then inexplicably leaves it out of his discussion of attitudes in *How We Think* (1933). I find the concept of directness to be useful and so include it here.

2. I accept Beverly Tatum's (1997) definition of racism as "a system involving cultural messages and institutional policies and practices as well as the beliefs and actions of individuals. [It is] a system that operates to the advantage of Whites and to the disadvantage of people of color" (p. 7).

3. Hemingway's short story "A Clean, Well-Lighted Place" refers to a clean, well-lit, orderly bar that offered a haven for an old man who recently had attempted suicide. In the helter-skelter that is life (including school), the kind of "known-ness" that such a space can offer can counter the darkness and potential threat of death, disorder, and dislocation that life pushes on the lives of so many of our students.

4. For the story of how I teach about the moon, Earth, and sun, see "Doing

Dewey" (Rodgers, 2015). For Eleanor's story of teaching the moon to her students, see "Teaching as Research" in *The Having of Wonderful Ideas* (Duckworth, 1987).

Part III

1. Dan Lortie (1975) called this the "apprenticeship of observation."
2. To my mind, "Any questions?" is the most inauthentic and unhelpful question a teacher can ask.
3. Some contemporary scholars (Nathan et al., 2014) call this "embodied cognition," which, as far as I can tell, is another term for interaction (Dewey, everything he ever wrote). Dancer and curriculum consultant Susan Griss, in the book *Minds in Motion* (Griss &Merecki, 1998), has written extensively about the use of movement and the body in learning.
4. For a lovely demonstration of each approach, visit bronxbetterlearning.org and scroll down to the video section.

Part IV

1. This process was first articulated by Claire Stanley, Jack Millet, and me at a TESOL conference in 1993. At the time we were all faculty in the Department of Language Teacher Education at the School for International Training (SIT) in Brattleboro, VT.
2. I am referring to the many wonderful colleagues with whom I have worked over the course of more than 3 decades at these institutions: SIT, La Guardia (NY) Community College, Vermont Insight Meditation Center, Antioch New England, the Bronx School for Better Learning, Marlboro College, and SUNY Albany.
3. www.youtube.com/watch?v=vJG698U2Mvo
4. The three books that make up the series are *The Golden Compass, The Amber Spyglass*, and *The Subtle Knife*.
5. You will recall that Argyris and Schön defined espoused theories as unassailable beliefs—how one would like to be perceived. Theories-in-use, on the other hand, lie beneath one's actual behaviors. They often go unexamined and, once apprehended, actually may surprise a person.
6. *Funds of knowledge* is a term coined by Luis Moll and his colleagues to denote the various and vast knowledge that comes from home, work in their parents' shops, stories of immigration, knowledge of politics and language, and so forth.
7. An earlier version of this section was published in the *Harvard Educational Review* (Rodgers, 2002) and is adapted here by permission.
8. I see analysis as the process of organizing data, and interpretation as the process of extracting meaning from these different arrangements. Different analyses, different interpretations.
9. Reflection on a word is a process developed by Patricia Carini and her colleagues to prepare the ground for descriptions of various kinds. It is meant to evoke certain associations, images, and memories that somehow speak to the person, institution, or issue at hand. For our group, the idea of the school as a home-like place provoked the reflection.
10. This process of descriptive inquiry follows those developed by Patricia Carini and her colleagues at the Prospect School in North Bennington, VT.
11. This flow from one focus to another—all connected—is an example of Dewey's concept of continuity in learning.
12. Cofounders of the Vermont Center for Insight Meditation in Brattleboro, VT.

13. The extent to which mindfulness practice attends to contextual forces and issues of social justice is beyond the scope of this book, and the knowledge of this author, but I believe it is an item of some discussion in the world of mindfulness practice. Certainly awareness of the social, political, economic, and historical forces, an explicit part of reflection, also would play a role in mindfulness practice.

Part V

1. Please share your responses to my work, questions, and suggestions at my website: albany.academia.edu/CarolRodgers/Community-Forum

2. From 2001 to 2006 my colleague Miriam Raider-Roth and I each taught a section of the course and conferred frequently on its contents, redesigning it each year. She still teaches a version of the course at the University of Cincinnati. We also coauthored the article out of which this book grew, "Presence in Teaching" (2006).

3. I read all students' posts, but do not respond individually to each one, although I do respond to some.

4. All work is shared with permission of the author and all names are either pseudonyms chosen by the author or their real names as requested by them.

5. From *Tell Me More*, edited by Eleanor Duckworth (2001).

6. Professor Agassiz unfortunately also became (in)famous for his work in "scientific racism," promoting the incorrect belief that intelligence and race are connected.

7. For a look at a sample album go to carolrodgers.academia.edu

8. And I confess that part of me also feels "bad" for what might be interpreted as "tricking" my students this way. But two things are at work. First, by this point in the course they have come to trust that my intentions are probably not of the "gotcha" kind. And second, the power of coming face-to-face with one's assumptions feels to me worth the risk.

9. I have written several articles on the process of descriptive feedback and its use as a part of reflection (Rodgers, 2002b; Rodgers, 2006; Rodgers & LaBoskey, 2016); as essential to presence in teaching (Rodgers & Raider-Roth, 2006); as a democratic process (Rodgers, 2010); and as practiced with elementary-level students (Rodgers, 2018).

10. The notion of an "understanding response" comes from the work of Carl Rogers, humanistic psychologist. In an interview he says, "From my point of view as therapist, I am not trying to 'reflect feelings.' I am trying to determine whether my understanding of the client's inner world is correct—whether I am seeing it as s/he is experiencing it at this moment. Each response of mine contains the unspoken question, 'Is this the way it is in you? Am I catching just the colour and texture and flavour of the personal meaning you are experiencing right now? If not, I wish to bring my perception in line with yours.'" cultureofempathy.com/References/Experts/Carl-Rogers.htm

11. I encourage readers to explore all of the books written by Carini and her colleagues, all published by Teachers College Press, and each growing out of the same philosophy of descriptive inquiry described here.

12. A Descriptive Review is different from an IEP report. (IEPs are required by U.S. federal law for all children with disabilities.) IEPs must focus on children's strengths as well as weaknesses, with the goal of "reducing or eliminating the child's problem. They should include ways to measure progress and be directly correlated to your child's identified disability." www.understandingspecialeducation.com/individualized-education-program.html

References

Adichie, C.N. (2009). *The danger of a single story*. Retrieved from www.ted.com /talks/chimamanda_ngozi_adichie_the_danger_of_a_single_story?language=en

Argyris, C., & Schön, D. (1974). *Theory in practice*. San Francisco, CA: Jossey-Bass.

Ball, D. L. (2018, April). *Just dreams and imperatives: The power of teaching in the struggle for public education*. Presidential address at the annual meeting of the American Educational Research Association, New York, NY.

Ball, D. L., & Forzani, F. M. (2007). What makes education research "educational"? *Educational Researcher, 36*(9), 529–540.

Brach, T. (2012). *True refuge: Finding peace and freedom in your own awakened heart*. New York, NY: Bantam Books.

Buber, M. (1987). *I and thou*. New York, NY: Macmillan. (Original work published 1923)

Cain, S. (2012). *Quiet*. New York, NY: Crown Publishing.

Canavesio, G. (Producer), & Ruspoli, T. (Director). (2010). *Being in the World*. [Motion picture]. U.S.A: Mangusta Productions.

Carini, P. F. (2001). *Starting strong*. New York, NY: Teachers College Press.

Carini, P. F. (2010). Making and doing philosophy in a school. In P. F. Carini & M. Himley, *Jenny's story* (pp. 154–166). New York, NY: Teachers College Press.

Charon, R. (2001). Narrative medicine: A model for empathy, reflection, profession, and trust. *Journal of the American Medical Association, 286*(15), 1897–1902).

Cochran-Smith, M., & Lytle, S. (1993). *Inside/out*. New York, NY: Teachers College Press.

Cochran-Smith, M., & Lytle, S. (Eds.). (2009). *Inquiry as stance*. New York, NY: Teachers College Press.

Coia, L., & Taylor, M. (2017). Let's stay in the swamp: Poststructural feminist reflective practice. In R. Brandenburg, K. Glasswell, M. Jones, J. Ryan (Eds.), *Reflective theory and practice in teacher education* (pp. 49–62). Singapore: Springer. doi:10.1007/978-981-10-3431-2_3

Cuban, L. (2013). *Inside the black box of classroom practice*. Cambridge, MA: Harvard Education Press.

Danielson, C. (2011). *The framework for teaching evaluation instrument*. Princeton, NJ: Danielson Group.

del Carmen Salazar, M. (2013). A humanizing pedagogy: Reinventing the principles and practice of education as a journey toward liberation. In C. Faltis & J. Abedi (Eds.), *Extraordinary pedagogies for working within school settings serving nondominant students* (Review of research in education, vol. 37, pp. 121–148). Washington, DC: AERA Publications.

Dewey, J. (1902). *The child and the curriculum*. Chicago, IL: University of Chicago Press.

Dewey, J. (1916). *Democracy and education*. New York, NY: Free Press.

Dewey, J. (1933). *How we think*. Buffalo, NY: Prometheus Books.

Dewey, J. (1934). *Art as experience*. New York, NY: Perigree Books.

Dewey, J. (1938). *Experience and education*. New York, NY: Touchstone.

Dickens, C. (2007). *Hard times*. New York, NY: Simon & Schuster. (Original work published 1854)

Dreyfus, H. L. (1991). *Being-in-the-world*. Cambridge, MA: MIT Press.

Dreyfus, H., & Wrathall, M. (Eds.). (2009). *A companion to phenomenology and existentialism*. Malden, MA: Wiley-Blackwell.

Duckworth, E. (1987). *The having of wonderful ideas*. New York, NY: Teachers College Press.

DuFour, R., & Eaker, R. (1998). *Professional learning communities at work*. Bloomington, IN: Solution Tree.

Fendler, L. (2003). Teacher reflection in a hall of mirrors: Historical influences and political reverberations. *Educational Researcher, 32*(3), 16–25.

Fenstermacher, G., & Richardson, V. (2005). On making determinations of quality in teaching. *Teachers College Record, 107*(1), 186–213.

Freire, P. (2011). *Pedagogy of the oppressed*. Boulder, CO: Westview Press. (Original work published 1970)

Gallwey, T. (1974). *The inner game of tennis*. New York, NY: Random House.

Gladwell, M. (2005). *Blink*. New York, NY: Little, Brown.

Goldstein, J. (2013). *Mindfulness: A practical guide to awakening*. Boulder, CO: Sounds True.

Goldstein, J. (2015, December 15). Mindfulness: What it is and is not [Video file]. Retrieved from www.youtube.com/watch?v=3Uqoxo_jPXQ

Greenblatt, S. (2011). *The swerve*. New York, NY: Norton.

Greene, M. (1977). Towards wide-awakeness. *Teachers College Record, 79*(1), 119–125.

Greene, M. (1978). *Landscapes of learning*. New York, NY: Alfred A. Knopf.

Greene, M. (1995). *Releasing the imagination*. San Francisco, CA: Jossey-Bass.

Griss, S., & Merecki, V. (1998). *Minds in motion*. Portsmouth, NH: Heinemann Press.

Groopman, J. (2007). *How doctors think*. New York, NY: Houghton Mifflin.

Hansen, D. (2004). A poetics of teaching. *Educational Theory, 54*(2), 119–142..

Hatano, G., & Inagaki, K. (1986). Two courses of expertise. In H. Stevenson, H. Azuma, & K. Hakuta (Eds.), *Child development and education in Japan* (pp. 262–272). New York, NY: W. H. Freeman.

Hawkins, D. (2000). *The roots of literacy*. Boulder, CO: University of Colorado Press.

Hawkins, D. (2002). I, thou, and it. In D. Hawkins, *The informed vision* (pp. 51–64). New York, NY: Algora Publishing. (Original work published 1974)

Himley, M. (with Carini, P.). (Eds.). (2000). *From another angle*. New York, NY: Teachers College Press.

Himley, M. (2010). Poiesis: Life on the uptake. In P. F. Carini & M. Himley, *Jenny's story* (pp. 143–153). New York, NY: Teachers College Press.

Hyde, L. (1983). *The gift*. New York, NY: Vintage Books.

Irving, D. (2014). *Waking up white*. Cambridge, MA: Elephant Room Press.

Kabat-Zinn, J. (2015, May 28). *John Kabat-Zinn me me me* [Video file]. Retrieved from www.youtube.com/watch?v=xeCXhXDkzpw

Kabat-Zinn, J. (2016). *Mindfulness for beginners: Reclaiming the present moment—and your life*. Boulder, CO: Sounds True.

Kahneman, D. (2011). *Thinking, fast and slow*. New York, NY: Farrar, Straus & Giroux.

Keet, A., Zinn, D., & Porteus, K. (2009). Mutual vulnerability: A key principle in a humanising pedagogy in post-conflict societies. *Perspectives in Education, 27*(2), 109–119.

Kegan, R. (1982). *The evolving self*. Cambridge, MA: Harvard University Press.

Kegan, R. (1994). *In over our heads: The mental demands of modern life*. Cambridge, MA: Harvard University Press.

Keller, E. F. (1983). *A feeling for the organism: The life and work of Barbara McClintock*. New York, NY: W.H. Freeman.

Kennedy, M. (2019). How we learn about teacher learning. *Review of Research in Education, 43*(1), 138–162.

Kincheloe, J. L. (2008). *Critical pedagogy primer*. New York, NY: Peter Lang.

Kolb, D. (1984). *Experiential learning*. New York, NY: Prentice Hall.

Lampert, M. (1985). How do teachers manage to teach? Perspectives on problems in practice. *Harvard Educational Review, 55*(2), 178–194.

Lampert, M., & Ball, D. L. (1999). Aligning teacher education with contemporary K–12 reform visions. In L. Darling-Hammond & G. Sykes (Eds.), *Teaching as the learning profession: Handbook of policy and practice* (pp. 33–53). San Francisco, CA: Jossey Bass.

Lortie, D. C. (1975). *Schoolteacher*. Chicago, IL: University of Chicago Press.

Lyons, N. (Ed.). (2010). *Handbook of reflection and reflective inquiry: Mapping a way of knowing for professional reflective inquiry*. New York, NY: Springer.

McDonald, J. (1992). *Teaching: Making sense of an uncertain craft*. New York, NY: Teachers College Press.

Moll, L. C., Amanti, C., Neff, D., & González, N. (1992). Funds of knowledge for teaching: A qualitative approach to connect households and classrooms. *Theory into Practice, 31*(2), 132–141.

Nathan, M. J., Walkington, C., Boncoddo, R., Pier, E., Williams, C. C., & Alibali, M. W. (2014). Actions speak louder with words: The roles of action and pedagogical language for grounding mathematical proof. *Learning and Instruction, 33*, 182–193.

Noddings, N. (1986). Fidelity in teaching, teacher education, and research for teaching. *Harvard Educational Review, 56*(4), 496–510.

Olendzki, A. (2016). *Untangling self*. Somerville, MA: Wisdom Publications.

Nussbaum, M. (2010). *Not for profit*. Princeton, NJ: Princeton University Press.

Poincaré, H. (1904). *Science and hypothesis*. London, England: The Walter Scott Publishing Co.

Pullman, P. (1996). *The golden compass*. New York, NY: Alfred A. Knopf.

Richert, A. (1992). Voice and power in teaching and learning to teach. In L. Valli (Ed.), *Reflective teacher education: Cases and critiques* (pp. 187–197). Albany: State University of New York Press.

Rodgers, C. (2002a). Defining reflection: Another look at John Dewey and reflective thinking. *Teachers College Record, 74*(4), 842–866.

Rodgers, C. (2002b). Seeing student learning: Teacher change and the role of reflection. *Harvard Educational Review, 72*(2), 230–253.

Rodgers, C. (2006a). "The turning of one's soul"— Learning to teach for social justice: The Putney Graduate School of Teacher Education (1950–1964). *Teachers
College Record, 108*(7), 1266–1295.

Rodgers, C. (2006b). Attending to student voice: The impact of descriptive feedback
on learning and teaching. *Curriculum Inquiry, 35*(2), 209–238.

Rodgers, C. R. (2010). The role of descriptive inquiry in building presence and civic
capacity. In N. Lyons (Ed.), *Handbook of reflective inquiry* (pp. 45–61). New
York, NY: Springer.

Rodgers, C. (2014). Doing Dewey. *Occasional Paper Series, 2014*(32). Retrieved
from educate.bankstreet.edu/occasional-paper-series/vol2014/iss32/8

Rodgers, C. (2018). Descriptive feedback: Students voice in K-5 classrooms. *Australian
Educational Researcher 45*(1), 87–102. doi.org/10.1007/s13384-018-0263-1

Rodgers, C., & LaBoskey, V. (2016). Reflective practice in teacher education. In J.
Loughran & M. L. Hamilton (Eds.), *International handbook of teacher education*, (Vol 2,.pp. 71–104). London, UK: Springer.

Rodgers, C., & Raider-Roth, M. (2006). Presence in teaching. *Teachers and Teaching: Theory and Practice, 12*(3), 265–287.

Rodgers, C., & Scott, K. (2008). Development of the personal self and profession-
al identity in learning to teach. In M. Cochran-Smith & S. Feiman-Nemser
(Eds.), *Handbook of research in teacher education* (pp. 732–754). Mahwah,
NJ: Earlbaum.

Sacks, O. (1995). To see and not see. In O. Sacks, *An anthropologist on Mars* (pp.
108–152). New York, NY: Vintage Books.

Sacks, O. (1999, December 20). Brilliant light. *The New Yorker.* pp. 56–73.

Sacks, O. (2019). *Everything in its place.* New York, NY: Alfred A. Knopf.

Salzberg, S. (2011). *Real happiness: The power of meditation.* New York, NY:
Workman Publishing.

Salzberg, S. (2019). Glossary. Retrieved from www.sharonsalzberg.com/glossary/

Schneier, L. (2001). Apprehending poetry. In E. Duckworth (Ed.), *Tell me more* (pp.
42–78). New York, NY: Teachers College Press.

Schoenfeld, A. (2014). What makes for powerful classrooms, and how can we support teachers in creating them? A story of research and practice, productively
intertwined. *Educational Researcher, 43*(8), 404–412.

Schön, D. (1983). *The reflective practitioner.* New York, NY: Basic Books.

Scudder, S. H. (1879). The student, the fish, and Agassiz: By the student. In *American poems* (3rd ed., pp. 450–454). Boston, MA: Houghton, Osgood & Co.
Retrieved from www.skidmore.edu/~mmarx/L&EF09/agassiz.pdf

Simons, D. & Chabris, C. (1999). The invisible gorilla. Retrieved from www
.theinvisiblegorilla.com/gorilla_experiment.html

Simons, D. (2011). *Seeing the world as it isn't.* Retrieved from www.youtube.com
/watch?v=9Il_D3Xt9W0

Swartz, T. (1978). On feedback. *Educational Solutions Newsletter*, pp. 5–10.

Tatum, B. (1997). *"Why are all the Black kids sitting together in the cafeteria?"* New
York, NY: Basic Books.

Zeichner, K., & Liston, D. (1996). *Reflective teaching: An introduction.* Mahwah,
NJ: Lawrence Erlbaum Assoicates.

Index

The letters *f* and *n* following a page number refer to a figure and a note, respectively.

About the Author

Carol R. Rodgers is an associate professor of education at the University at Albany, State University of New York. Her work has focused on reflective practice, the educational philosophy of John Dewey, presence in teaching, the theory and practice of a humanizing pedagogy, the history of progressive teacher education, and processes of descriptive inquiry. She has taught English as a Foreign Language (EFL) in Sénégal as a Peace Corps volunteer; been an EFL teacher trainer at Galang and Phanat Nikhom Refugee Camps in Southeast Asia (Indonesia and Thailand); and consulted in teacher education and teacher professional development in the United States, Japan, South Africa, Brazil, and Canada. From 1985 to 2000 she was a professor at the School for International Training (SIT) in Brattleboro, Vermont. In 2011 she was a Fulbright Senior Scholar at Nelson Mandela University in Port Elizabeth, South Africa. She lives in Amherst, Massachusetts, with her husband and her dog, Mozart.